Title-

The Dominant Force:

How to multiply profits, dominate your field and earn the respect you deserve.

Introduction

Successful entrepreneurs constantly do these three things:
1 Identifying prospects who want what they are selling
2 Attracting those specific prospects
3 Converting them into customers with an irresistible offer

The next phase is Growth which means:
1 Increasing the number of customers you have
2 Increasing the transaction size per sale
3 Getting those customers to keep coming back

That's the easy part:
Growing that into a formidable empire is where entrepreneurs struggle.

New entrepreneurs usually start businesses because they want freedom, wealth and a way to impact the world.

After their businesses are established, they seek an empire.

They want respect, recognition, influence and global relevance.

They want to become The Dominant Force in their industry.

You will understand how men like David Oyedepo, Andrew Carnegie and John D Rockefeller built their empires.

This book discusses how to grow a business to that level of global relevance.

You will learn proven business growth strategies as well as how to influence people.

Most importantly, you will learn how to use faith and wisdom to develop power and influence.

After all, a person with influence and no power can easily be defeated.

Of all the things you will do in your life and business this year, only a few are worth doing.

By worth doing-I mean only a few things will give you the greatest outcomes.

Why would anyone bother to do things that are a waste of time?

The answer is that most people don't know which activities will bring them the greatest returns.

They don't know which pillars, strategies, tactics or employees are responsible for their highest growth.

This book is about upside leverage and using mental triggers to attract people and increase sales.

Doing the few things that bring the greatest results.

You will learn that a business that has a clear focus + a deep understanding of the market + consistent implementation is almost impossible to beat unless through negligence.

What is your focus?

What deep understanding is driving your business?

Do you consistently implement strategies and send out offers to your prospects?

What is upside leverage?

The amount of increase or improved results you can get an action or activity to produce for you.

The best way to understand some of what I'll be sharing is to see how I applied it to my business.

This is how we will start this adventure.

P.S Brace yourself for colloquialism. This isn't a textbook. It's a practical guide. Anything you find repetitive was written on purpose.

Pick the meat and discard with the bones.

© 2016 JEFFREY MANU
All rights reserved. No portion of this book may be reproduced, stored in a retrieval system, or transmitted in any form or by any means—electronic, mechanical, photocopy, recording, scanning, or other—except for brief quotations in critical reviews or articles, without the prior written permission of the publisher.
Published in San Jose, California by GrowingStartup, LLC.

Table of Contents

1. Get A Clear Vision Of Where You Are Going
2. Focus
3. The Highest Value Customer
4. Positioning: What do they say about you?
5. Education in Marketing and Instant gratification
6. The weapon of Instant Gratification
7. Social proof, testimonials and case studies
8. Setting Big Goals and Hitting Them
9. Multiplying your profits with fewer clients and less stress
10. Automated Business Growth Systems That Turn Marketing into Profit
11. A simple formula to make sure your foundation is right
12. 8 ways to increase revenue growth
13. Product Launch Case Study
14. Influence and Persuasion As Marketing Magnets
15. Psychological Triggers That Attract, Inspire and Motivate People
16. Hiring and Culture
17. Business don't sign checks. Humans do.
18. How To Write Magnetic Sales Letters
19. How to Create A Moneymaking Webinar
20. The Loaded Presentation Variation
21. How to Create Videos That Make Money
22. The Unlimited Life
23. Epilogue
24. Bonuses

1

Get a Clear Vision of Where You Are Going

To become the dominant force in your market, you are going to have to discover what your calling is.

What group of people were you created to serve?

What do you enjoy doing that energizes you regardless of how much you are paid?

Everyone was created with at least one dominant gift, message, passion, vision and mission in life.

God already gave each of us the formula to follow in Genesis 1

[28] And God blessed them, and God said unto them, Be fruitful, and multiply, and replenish the earth, and subdue it: and have dominion over the fish of the sea, and over the fowl of the air, and over every living thing that moveth upon the earth.

First we are to bear fruit. You may have a song in you, an idea for an innovative widget, a message that the entire world needs to hear or a formula that will change how stocks are traded globally. That idea is a seed that has to be converted into fruit so it can bless mankind.

Second, we are to take that fruit, business, music, art, innovation and multiply (distribute) it to as many people as we can. Once the seed is turned into fruit, the world has to be blessed by it. It is selfishness to keep your fruit to just a few people.

Third, we are to develop that product, message or service into other forms or channels that will make it increase in value. Innovation is multiplying the value of what you currently have.

Finally, God gives us the charge and ability to subdue and have dominion over this earth. He was very careful not to say we should have dominion over other people. That is bondage.

Dominion over all the earth means to cover this world with your value. The discovery of modern day marvels such as electricity, aviation, the internet and television have moved the human race exponentially forward.

Imagine if only ten percent of the world's population had the internet. A lot of development in government, education and business wouldn't be where it is today.

Now that you are clear on your vision, you have to align everything you do to achieve that goal.

John D. Rockefeller famously said that his vision was to light the world.

In his case, the fruit of choice was by building the most successful oil refining empire of his time (and arguably of all time.)

Walt Disney wanted to "make people happy."

He chose to use stories, film, animation, experiences and entertainment to do this.

Identify your primary calling and give it all you've got.

Ask yourself, "What is my life's work going to be?"

At age 80, what will you say you spent your life doing?

What fruit will you say you created, multiplied, distributed and impacted the world with?

Part of discovering your calling is to find out where you have an edge and develop that skill, mindset or gift.

It is folly to try to do anything that you can't become a master at.

I recommend that you write down things you do that produce effortless results.

Next, develop each of those gifts till you know which one you have intuitive mastery at and focus on that one.

E.g. one of my mentors, David Oyedepo says he is called to "Liberate the World from All Oppressions of the Devil through the Preaching of the Word of Faith "

Write down your primary vision on this earth? What will your life's work be? What is your calling?

What is that thing that you do better than anyone else?

What do you see that others don't?

What seeds has God given you?

You may have spent twenty years doing the wrong thing. It's not too late to do what you were created to do.

2 FOCUS

But ONE THING I do: Forgetting what is behind and straining toward what is ahead… Philippians 3:13 (emphasis mine)

"I'm no genius. I'm smart in spots—but I stay around those spots."
- Tom Watson Sr., Founder of IBM

"What an investor needs is the ability to correctly evaluate selected businesses. Note that word "selected": You don't have to be an expert on every company, or even many. You only have to be able to evaluate companies within your circle of competence. The size of that circle is not very important; knowing its boundaries, however, is vital."-Warren Buffett

"You have to figure out what your own aptitudes are. If you play games where other people have the aptitudes and you don't, you're going to lose. And that's as close to certain as any prediction that you can make. You have to figure out where you've got an edge. And you've got to play within your own circle of competence.

If you want to be the best tennis player in the world, you may start out trying and soon find out that it's hopeless—that other people blow right by you. However, if you want to become the best plumbing contractor in Bemidji, that is probably doable by two-thirds of you. It takes a will. It takes the intelligence. But after a while, you'd gradually know all about the plumbing business in Bemidji and master the art. That is an attainable objective, given enough discipline. And people who could never win a chess tournament or stand in center court in a respectable tennis tournament can rise quite high in life by slowly developing a circle of competence—which results partly from what they were born with and partly from what they slowly develop through work."—Charlie Munger

The apostle Paul said he was focused on doing ONE THING.

Having a singular focus is what separates those who get results from the rest of the world.

Do you know what it feels like to spend 12 hours at work and still feel like you could have been more productive?

Research shows that distractions are one of the biggest problems plaguing the business world.

A lot of people show up for work but few of those hours are actually used to do productive work.

The rest of the time is full of distractions such as phone calls, emails, unnecessary meetings, phone notifications and social media.

Many of your business challenges would be solved if you knew how to focus on one thing at a time.

The media likes to idolize people who are running several businesses at the same time.

I heard once such billionaire talk about his day and his schedule was surprising.

He said all he did at his other businesses was answer emails.

Most of his attention, energy and resources were on one business.

Entrepreneurs have this habit of doing too many things at the same time.

The top performers think and act differently.

The most influential business owners focus till it hurts.

They know how to focus their time, energy, emotions and resources on only one project at a time.

Once your vision and calling are well defined, you have to decide to focus.

Choose to do only the few things that will bring you the greatest results.

Force yourself not to diversify your attention or resources.

If you are launching a product in 2 months, don't waver and try to work on other things that can wait.

Don't be waiting in line at the bank or doing dry cleaning errands during the day.

If it's not making you money or creating value for your customers, don't do it.

In life and business, there are a few things that matter.

The rest of the stuff that seems pressing are usually things that will not have any crucial long term impact on the business.

You need to stick to your vision and give it all you've got.

There are very few people who can successfully do more than one thing or be engaged in more than one venture at a time.

What's the solution?

Focus your time on uninterrupted blocks working on only high priority activities.

High priority activities are the ones which will matter most to the growth of your business.

For many entrepreneurs the only things they should be doing are Strategic planning, marketing and Sales.

Depending on the business, you may have to keep doing the value creation but if you don't have to, train someone else to do it.

Even though hiring, answering emails and others are important, they can be taught and systemized.

My advice for you is to set your agenda in such a way that you can work a full 90 minutes without distraction.

Whatever emails or phone calls that come during that hour can be dealt with when you are done.

This simple productivity tip will show help you budget your time better.

I also know people who check their email and notifications immediately they wake up.

What they are unintentionally doing is allowing the world to control how they invest their time.

They react instead of being proactive.

My email and notifications are usually the answered about 2 to 3 hours after I wake up.

In all my years I have never woken up to an emergency that couldn't be solved later.

What's going to be the focus of your business for the next 12 months?

Write it here:………………………………………………………………..

For example, "We are going to grow our customer base by 2 million in 12 months."

"We are going to launch a beauty brand in Ghana."

"We are going to increase the sales of product X by 70% in 12 months."

P.S The most important thing you should do every day is personal development. By this I mean spiritually, mentally and physically.

The highest value customer

The customer you understand the best is your highest value customer. The minute that customer feels that you are the one who understands them the most, you become their highest perceived source of value."

Perception and Empathy matter more than most people know.

In your market, I'm sure you know of some shady businesses that seem to be prospering.

This is partly because customers perceive them to be a good source of value.

Let's talk about your market.

We are focusing on your customers and the goods and services you sell.

Which kind of customer in your market do you understand the most?

Someone once said, "People don't just buy from you because you understand them. They buy from you because they feel understood."

The person who "gets you", is the one who wins your approval.

Does your customer think you understand her?

Defining the best customer

The best customer is someone who is actively looking for what you are selling, has the ability to pay for it and has a recent purchase history of something similar to what you provide or even the same thing.

The last part is important because a prospect who has already bought from your competitor in the past already understands the benefits of your product.

He may not know of what makes you different but it's easier to convert a prospect who already understands the value of your offer.

When I run Lightcreative, I found out that clients who had already dealt with a competitor in the past were easier to convert.

They already know the benefits of the service and they were just looking for the best.

On the other hand, clients who needed education and explanation were usually tougher to convert.

One strategy I teach my students and clients on growing their businesses exponentially is this.

Find out the inactive clients of your competitor's and offer them your goods and services.

It would surprise you how many of them are probably looking for someone like you.

Part of the reason this works is that it's likely that your competitors have poor follow-up sequences.

You can take advantage of their sloppiness and become the dominant player in your field.

Here are some questions you should sit with your team and answer today.

Which customers in your market are looking for what you can provide?

Are there prospects out there who urgently want what I'm selling?

Are there prospects eagerly looking for my product?

Which of them have bought from a competitor in the last 18 months?

Do they perceive the current alternatives are few or inadequate?

4

Positioning: what do they say about you?

The diamond engagement ring industry was created from the ground up

Imagine one of your best clients is at a dinner party and mentions your name to a friend. The friend is looking for the product or solution you provide. That friend asks, "How are they different from the others?"

Will she say, "They are the landscaper who can process your application, give you a quote and be at your house in 2 hours?"

Or "He is the only financial advisor who has deep expertise in helping trust fund baby's manager their wealth."

Or "She is the only copywriter who understands how to write copy for baby products that causes mothers to buy."

Unfortunately people think of positioning as positioning a product when the strategy means to positioning a message in your prospects mind.

It's finding a niched message that will help your prospects identify and separate you from your competition.

If you are just starting a new business or launching a new product, it's best to have a message that niche's you to one customer segment.

I like how the fashion world positioned the message of jeans.

Even though the fabric is the same, nearly every brand has their own line of jeans.

There are jeans you can wear to the office, jeans that are worn by people who do manual labor and jeans that are for daily casual wear.

How does your customer think of you?

5

Education in Marketing and Instant gratification

On October 19, 1948, Merrill Lynch published a 6,450 word ad in the New York Times. It cost them about five thousand dollars to run the ad which Louis Engel convinced his bosses was a good idea.

The ad had no explicit references to the brokerage firm and was blandly titled, "What Everybody Ought to Know about This Stock and Bond Business"

At the bottom, the bottom right of the page was a little call to action that acknowledge Merrill Lynch as the sponsor and invited the reader to request free reprints of the ad in pamphlet form.

Engel who had only been at the firm for two years, gave his superiors two major concerns.

First, such free information and education was sure to benefit their rivals.

Secondly, why would anyone respond to getting a pamphlet of something they could simple tear out of the paper?

Before I share with you the results, it's important to note that Merrill Lynch first tested this concept in a smaller publication in Cleveland.

This is important because testing is important before you invest heavily in any campaign or promotion.

Back to the story…

The Cleveland experiment had encouraging results.

After Engel published his ad in the New York Times, Merrill Lynch received more than five thousand requests from potential customers.

What's amazing is that they received hundreds of long and thoughtful letters from appreciative readers.

One person said: "God bless Merrill Lynch; …I have been wanting to know this all my life;…I owned stocks and bonds and I never really knew what I owned."

The firm run the same promotion, or slightly edited versions, in newspapers across the country for the next few months and years.

They are said to have received over three million responses and millions of customers.

You can imagine the impact such an ad had on their business.

Decades later, Merrill Lynch is a part of Bank of America and manages of over $2.2 trillion in client assets.

Do you think this will work today?

Have you heard of Ogilvy and Mather?

David Ogilvy modeled Louis Engel's approach and created 17 ads for his business.

In one report David Ogilvy said he had sold over 1.4 billion dollars' worth of advertising.

Would you like to know how to use these same strategies to increase your market share?

Make it a focus to educate your market better than any competitor can.

The better advised a person is, the more likely they are to hold you in high regard as an expert.

The weapon of Instant Gratification

First impressions matter in how people use products.

If the first few minutes of a show do not engage you, it's likely that you will look for something else to watch.

The music industry does this really well.

The artist releases her best single before trying to sell the album.

If the first single becomes a hit, the album usually does well.

Why doesn't the promotion lead with any other track on the album?

Artists understand the principle of instant gratification.

It's the same principle that food vendors use when they give out samples.

They know the samples will make you think the rest of the food is good.

You should always put your best foot forward in a campaign or promotion.

On your website, in your retail space or during a presentation, start with the thing that will help move your customer towards their desired outcome.

In my coaching and consulting business, we are able to target million dollar clients by offering them a free campaign that should give them at least $10,000 if done right.

Why do we do this instead of charging them for it?

The client who is able to use one of our campaigns to increase their income will automatically start wondering what else we have to offer.

This simple strategy is ninety percent of our sales pitch without even looking like a sales pitch.

I always tell students that great marketing is when the prospect thinks they came up with the buying decision on their own.

People like to buy things. They just don't want to think that someone else made the decision for them.

My advice to service based businesses is that you should offer an important part of your value as a free trial.

For product businesses, samples work really well.

Even better is risk reversal where a client can purchase the product and return it anytime they want because it's backed by a full money back guarantee.

Think of this as the trailer to your movie.

Make it great and you will fill the seats.

Social proof, testimonials and case studies

18 And when He got into the boat, he who had been demon-possessed begged Him that he might be with Him. 19 However, Jesus did not permit him, but said to him, "Go home to your friends, and tell them what great things the Lord has done for you, and how He has had compassion on you." 20 And he departed and began to proclaim in Decapolis all that Jesus had done for him; and all marveled. Mark 5:18-20

There is an important marketing strategy mentioned here.

The backstory of this account is that Jesus had delivered a man of demons a few verses earlier.

As Jesus was departing, the man wanted to join Him.

Jesus' response was interesting.

He sent the man out to the Decapolis region. From what I have read, this was a federation of ten cities.

Deka = ten and polis = city. This was also an area greatly influenced by Greek culture.

The Bible says this new evangelist went about proclaiming what Jesus had done and all marveled.

Jesus is teaching us how to use social proof as a way to attract customers.

Businesses still use social proof, testimonials and case studies to make billions of dollars.

This works because when someone you know recommends a product or experience, you are more likely to want the same thing.

There are entire corporations whose growth has skyrocketed because of the viral loops that these kinds of testimonials, recommendations and endorsements create.

In January 2000, Subway launched a campaign based on a young man who had lost 200 pounds by eating their sandwiches.

The brand made him a spokesman for close to 15 years and according to one article this was responsible for one third to half of Subway's growth in the 15 year period. (It's sad but interesting to note that Subway had to cut ties with this spokesman after he was found to have engaged in criminal activities. This is a cautionary tale for all businesses to heed.)

If you can find or create a spokesperson with such a compelling story, do it.

Empathy may be the most important word in business

Social proof and endorsements also show that your business has empathy.

Many prospects see a product but are not sure if it's right for them.

Another rarely mentioned advantage of this is that depending on the product, we prefer to buy from someone we have a connection with.

Farmers will feel more comfortable buying insurance from an agent who has lived on a farm.

The weight loss industry consistently uses before-and-after photos to show how well their solutions work.

You can do that too.

In your marketing, show images of people who have tried your products and seen results.

Something as simple as photos of past clients goes a long way in making prospects more likely to buy from you.

What forms of social proof, endorsements and testimonials can you promote today?

8 Setting Big Goals and Hitting Them

When I was 17, I worked 12 hour days as a business to business salesman.

It was a purely commission based job so I only got paid if I sold something.

Every morning at 7 am, we would be given a bag full of different items such as pens, maps, toys, watches and whatever doohickey they could come up with.

Of all the items we sold, it is the London A to Z maps that I remember the most.

One thing you learn quickly when you are a salesperson in a new city is that many of the residents either can't give you good directions or are as clueless as you are.

I hadn't been in London for more than 3 months so I needed to know exactly where my prospects were even before we left the office.

The other salespeople would ignore the map and trust their ignorance to help them find our prospects.

There was no Google Maps or IPhone at the time so finding little known small businesses was a herculean task.

Another thing that made me appreciate step by step instructions was our early morning meetings.

At the briefing, a salesperson who had conquered a certain zone would have tips on which buyers in that neighborhood were more likely to pay and what tactics to use to close the sale.

Some business owners preferred if you showed up in a suit.

Others were more eager to buy from someone who wore a t-shirt and jeans.

One business owner liked me because he liked my Prada shoes. (They were actually my uncle's and I only wore them because I didn't have black sneakers.)

Having sales targets, a map to find the prospect's location and having a step by step blueprint to attract customers and make the sale are lessons that have helped me build a successful profitable business today.

Most business owners don't know how to set and achieve business goals.

In fact, many don't even know what the goals are so they don't have any way to measure how successful the business is.

Eagles don't define success as being able to fly higher than a chicken.

You shouldn't compare yourself to your competitors and neither should you base your growth targets on last year's results.

Think about the most successful person you know.

Using money as our measure, you may say that person has $80 billion dollars but what if their potential was to make $200 billion?

This is why you need your own inner score card as Warren Buffett calls it.

What vision has God put in your heart?

I'm always a bit saddened when young people use their parent's as their benchmark or starting point.

The only benchmark necessary is the potential that God has given us.

That potential is infinite.

Faith is reality.

Faith isn't hope or expectation.

Faith is living in your desires before they manifest.

There are memes and quotes about scaling mountains, pushing down obstacles and so on.

In truth, faith doesn't even consider those obstacles.

Part of the reason I'm successful is because I don't see the obstacles. I'm too high above them to care.

I'd like to force you to see that no man is a factor to how high you can go or how big you can grow.

With the ability of God that you have in you, nothing can stand in your way.

I tell people all the time that money is a currency for natural men.

With the name of Jesus and faith, there is nothing you lack in this life.

With that mindset, do this exercise

Decide on where you want to go and then you will know what it takes to get there.

1 12 months from today, I will have this amount of revenue

……………………………………………………………………………
……………..

2 12 months from today, my business will have grown by this percentage

……………………………………………………………………………
……………..

3 12 months from today, we would have sold this number of products/services

....
....

4 12 months from today, I will have this percentage of my market as my customers (write down market-share goal)

....
....

5 Write the vision-3 years from today, I will have the following lifestyle.
For example, I work 5 days of the week and I don't have to work 12 hours a day because I have systems in place that grow the business even when I'm not physically in the office. I work with clients that I love and our profits are up 50% from last month.

We have 70% market share and our business is growing at a pace that we can control. Our bills are paid and we are not slaves to any banks or lenders. I have lunch every day at a fancy restaurant of my choice. My family is happy and I am loved by my spouse and children.

My community and the marketplace see and praise me for my contribution to the business world. I have the freedom to do what I want and be creative in my business without worrying about breaking anything. I go on beautiful vacations with my family and never have to think about work because the systems in place are working.

I am respected in my industry and many people call on me for advice. My staff is excited to come to work every day and they even tell their friends how wonderful it is to work here. I have all the cars, homes and assets I desire.

....
....

Those who do not know where they are going do not know how far they are from their desires

9
Multiplying your profits with fewer clients and less stress

In telling my story, I'm going to make a strong case for why focus, faith and wisdom should be important to you.

Let's start with the questions entrepreneurs often ask me:

Q1-What is the biggest cause of slow growth for business owners?

Overwhelm and a lack of focus.

Most business owners are doing too many things at the same time and not focusing on what will produce the highest upside and leverage.

Q2 What are the simple solutions for busy entrepreneurs?

You can cure overwhelm with these simple steps.

(Interestingly both the Harvard Business Review and the Stanford News Service have spent a lot of time researching this.)

Step 1 You have to understand where you are now.

Write down how much money your business has brought you in the last 12 months.

Step 2 I'd like you to calculate what your rudimentary expenses are.
For e.g. house payments, children, gas, cars etc.
Successful businesses bring in at least 8 times whatever the monthly expenses are.

At least. Anything else is unacceptable.

Step 3 Where do you want to be?
Hypothetically let's say you made $2.5m after taxes last year.

In the next 2 years you want to double that figure to $5m.

Step 4 What will it cost you to get there?
This is where you do an appraisal of what your highest growth drivers are.

The wise thing to do next is to double down on those drivers and optimize them so that you reap more than what you spend in Marketing and Advertising.

If you were not satisfied after this short exercise, it means you are probably not the dominant force or celebrated authority in your field. This is where I usually educated the person on our Dominant Entrepreneur program.

Q3-What do you do?
I set up campaigns and promotions for entrepreneurs who sell premium products and services.

I'm the founder of Growingstartup.com; a media and technology company focused on helping entrepreneurs grow businesses.

Q4-How do you make money?
Clients pay me to build campaigns and promotions for them.

They pay me a fixed amount plus royalties on the profits of the campaign.

Secondly, I hold monthly workshops for entrepreneurs who are in the consulting business or involved in high-consultative selling at high fees or transaction sizes, (such as real estate, investments, financial advisory services, software etc.)….

Or are in the business/life/sales coaching business (such as coaching/mastermind groups, practice management, etc.)…

Q4b What has driven your business' growth?
These 3 pillars were and are still the greatest drivers of my growth

1 Identify and attract high value, high paying clients.

2 Only do the most productive activities to help them.

3 Convert more of them with an automated Content Marketing system.

Q5- What does your sales sequence look like?
This is the exact sales sequence that took me from struggling business owner to respected authority.

1 Create a lead magnet that demonstrates value.

2 Deploy an offer that takes away risk and promises more value.

3 Close the sale by using mental triggers to convert the prospect.

Q6- What are the 3 main traffic sources you use?

1 Leverage via joint ventures, collaborations and affiliates

2 High Impact Appearances, speaking engagements and workshops

3 Highly Targeted Advertising campaigns

Q7- What is your best advice when it comes to pricing?

Your price should always be a discount of the value you are selling. For example, my fee starts at $50,000 because I can help a successful business owner make $500,000.

Q8- What books do you recommend for growing a business?

- Titan by Ron Chernow
- The Bible (from the Book of Acts to Hebrews)
- Success Systems by David Oyedepo
- Signposts On The Road To Success by E.W Kenyon
- Made In America by Sam Walton

Why I Am Sharing My Secrets

I started my first business in Ghana with zero capital and today I am blessed to be able to charge fees of $50,000.

I know a lot of business owners who are working all the time, losing sleep, precious family time and have little to show for their labor.
I hope my story will do two things.

First, it will not only inspire but give you a step by step road map to finally living the life you dream of.

Secondly, whenever I share my story,

I attract clients and students who want me to help them achieve the same results.

At the end of this presentation I'll offer you a chance to do the same.

Part 1-Humble Beginnings

My journey to fortune includes selling Valentine's Day cards and cellphones in high school to-

- *selling sunglasses door to door on the streets of England at 17*
- *starting and growing a T shirt printing business and Artisan Management firm in Ghana*
- *building one of Africa's first IOS apps in 2008*
- *selling handmade shoes*
- *running a branding and design firm*
- *teaching a STEM workshop for African youth*
- *running a Consulting and Professional services firm in Silicon Valley*
- *building the world's first mobile strategy game for Entrepreneurs*

Working All the Time, With Little to Show For It- And Not Enjoying Life

This is for you if you know your business could grow faster if only you knew what to do.

This is also my story on how my professional services business is able to charge up to $50,000 a day per client.

We literally went from charging $500 a month to $15,000 a month and then $50,000 a day in less than 14 months.

No new offices. No fancy letterheads. No new website.

The only thing that changed was my perspective-and I'll walk you through how to grow your business

Before we begin, here are the biggest mistakes I've made in my career

1 Choosing the wrong clients

2 Charging the wrong price

3 Not knowing how to create a good offer and closing the sale

The good news is that I'll teach you how I turned my business around in 10 months.

My biggest secrets are-

1. Faith- I literally moved from charging $500 to $50,000 by believing that I could do it and then I acted on that belief. It will surprise you that the top 10 percent of successful entrepreneurs and business owners in this world aren't necessarily smarter. Success stands behind the door of boldness.
2. Choosing the right customer.
3. Giving customers more value than they paid for.

   It's that simple.

   I haven't met a single struggling business owner who has a strategic vision and a plan to get there.

   Most people focus on traffic tactics, promotional gimmicks and generally copying anything they can see someone else doing.

All of the above have merit but without a strategic system, you will likely retire from your busy working life knowing you could have achieved more.

Part 2-Creating Value on the Way to Fortune

Question 1-

I asked myself, "Of all the things I know how to do, which of these activities energize me the most?

- One on one consulting and training
- Group coaching and training of Entrepreneurs on Business Growth and Marketing Strategy
- Building Done-for-you Marketing Campaigns, Back-end systems and Sales Sequences

At the time I decided to focus on building Done-for-you Marketing Campaigns, Back-end systems and Sales sequences.

Identifying my highest value clients

Question 2- How much do I want to be paid per client?

I already knew that my work was making my clients a lot of money but I had to decide on who to give my attention to.

This is not "how much can the client pay?"
That is not important at this point.
You have to decide on what you want first.
I chose an average client fee of $10,000 a month plus royalties.

I chose this also because I help clients make three to four times what they pay me. If the client can logically see that you are giving them more than they are paying, they will gladly pay more.

Question 3-Which of my client profiles would I love to be friends with and which of them is most committed to their success?

This question is important because it's best to work with people who you can call friends.

When I started out, I had clients that I didn't even want to talk to. They were just a pain in the neck and no matter how much they paid, it didn't take away the fact that I wasn't happy working with them.

I chose the client type that I could relate to. The kind of person I could share book and movie recommendations with. The kind of client I would invite home for dinner with my family.

For me this is an Entrepreneur or business owner as opposed to a corporation.

Secondly I also wanted someone who was ambitious and a quick implementer.

I'm sure you know what it's like to work with someone who is not committed to getting results and is always making excuses. The excuse I disliked the most was, "this will not work in my industry."

Finally, I decided to work with only those kinds of clients who I knew were motivated and willing to pay for my services. I chose people who I could get results for even with my eyes closed.

> Today this is a description of my average client- John runs his own business with a customer base of 70,000 or more people. He sells high ticket and high profit products and services. His website has about 10,000 unique visits every month. He wants to be in top 3 businesses in his industry and would like to be among the Forbes top 10. He reads books, believes in God and loves creating value for his customers. John spends thousands of dollars on Marketing and Advertising every month and wants to make a profit. John is married with two children that he loves dearly and wants to spend more time at home on the weekends. John wants to build an empire that has global relevance.

Question 3- Which 3 things can I do for John that will give him quick and consistent results?

1 Help him identify the right high paying customer base and the activities that are bringing in the most results.

2 Help him develop and promote an offer to attract the right customers.

3 Help him develop and execute a system that uses mental triggers to convert his prospects into customers

4 Help him re-activate past customers by creating residual and repeat sales.

Question 4- How much do I want to make in a year and how many clients will I need to achieve that?

At the time I wanted to make $10 million so I only needed 8 or 9 clients to achieve that.

How Do I Attract Clients to This Offer and What Is My Sales Sequence

Here is what my sales system looks like

1 Traffic through: Appearances, Advertising or Joint ventures (Partnerships and Affiliate Promotion) in the form of online Ad, direct mail, content etc.

2 Opt-in via an online squeeze page to collect email and name (some say your conversion rates go up if you only give the visitor one space to fill)

3 Prospect reads sales letter or video

What your competitors are doing wrong

- They are more focused on traffic instead of conversion. They think awareness, likes and popularity are the path to consistent wealth. Traffic is not the same as conversion.
- They are targeting everyone instead of focusing on the right customers.
- They are doing a lot so they don't know which of their activities bring in the most results.
- They copy whatever they see someone else do without understanding the process.

What I am teaching you to do is different because it

- Puts the focus on the client and not you.
- Focuses on getting high quality leads.
- Removes the need for traditional sales
- Positions and differentiates you in the eyes of your market because they know what your USP and Value Proposition are.

Part 3-Building the System

Step 1-Building Lead Magnets

I read E.W Kenyon's Hidden Man and it opened my eyes.

He explained how most college graduates were failures because they had been given information but lacked wisdom.

They knew where to go but didn't know how to get there.

I saw that all the business failures around me, including mine were a result of a lack of wisdom.

My clients wanted to pay for results and not information.

For example, information is when you tell a CEO that he needs better sales sequences to increase his customer lifetime value.

Wisdom is when you give him the sales sequences to implement.

People want to pay for results.

I started trading wisdom and I did this with my lead magnets.

What you are looking at now is a lead magnet. I'm giving you wisdom for free and showing you exactly how to use it.

Your prospect or lead magnet will attract the perfect clients and make them respond to answer all questions and dissolve all doubts.

The way to do this effectively is to write down every question, objection and fear that your prospect may have.

Next, answer each one of those objections in your lead magnets so they have no reason to doubt you.

Examples of lead magnets I use are eBooks, special reports, free presentations, free consulting, free trials, samples etc.

Step 2-Creating and Promoting an Offer That They Can't Refuse

What I did next was to offer to give free help to qualified prospects.

As long as you fit my criteria, I would show you how to use Marketing Strategy and Sales Growth Systems to grow your business.

My offer is—Would you like me to build a customized Growth System and Marketing Campaign for you?

Here is what made my offer effective:

- I showed them the benefits— "I will help you come up with a solid plan to increase revenue by building systems that attract new customers, reactivate past customers and get them spending again. I will also show you a simple strategy to add back-end revenue, develop joint ventures partnerships and increase word of mouth. "

People pay for results not features.

- I was transparent about my reasons for sharing— "The reason I'm doing this is simple. I enjoy working with successful entrepreneurs and helping ambitious business owners grow their businesses. Secondly doing this attracts new leads who can pay for my services which start at $10,000/m or $50,000 a day."

- I took away their sales fear— "This is not a sales pitch in disguise. At the end of this presentation, you may consider working with me. "

Why? Contrary to popular belief, telling the truth and honesty is a better tool for customer acquisition than deception. If you don't tell people why you are doing something free for them, their minds tend to think you have an ulterior motive. In my case, my motive is always mutually beneficial so I say it.

- I gave them an offer by reversing the risk—" If you use my system, book or attend a workshop and are not satisfied with your results simply email me and I'll return your deposit. You can even keep the entire system for free at that point. You have nothing to lose."

The reason I give such an outrageous guarantee is that I don't want fear of risk to stop someone from doing the right thing. By taking away the risk, the prospect feels more confident and know they have nothing to lose.

- I defined my perfect client– "For this to be of great benefit to you, I believe you must fit the following criteria ….."

This is where I tell them that I only work with Entrepreneurs and people who run either product or service based businesses.

I tell them how I like to work with Entrepreneurs, Marketers, Professional Services businesses such as Accounting firms, Legal Services, Healthcare Service providers, Real Estate Lessors, Investment Firms, Holding Companies.

I explain that my qualifying process includes website, list size, previous year's sales volume, sales goals, biggest roadblock today, and Marketing/Advertising budget.

I usually use Typeform to collect this information.

Step 3-
A Close-Ended Call to Action
- I reiterate what is in it for them

"'Here is what this system gives you- A highly targeted segment of responsive prospects who know what your offer is, how much you charge and why they should do business with you. What's great about this is that they actually want to contact you to help them now.

If this sounds like you I would like to know more about you so I can be best prepared to help you when we speak. Please click the link below to schedule a planning session with me. You will see a form with a few questions about your business and what you're looking to achieve. This will help me do market research and set up a time for us to go over the plan together."

The link they click takes them to the form I mentioned where they have to qualify themselves to speak with me.

I then do research on the client to find out if what they say is true. Most importantly I want to know if they have goodwill in their market. It's more difficult to get customers to buy when they don't like the business.

It's after this that I schedule an interview with them using Google Calendar.

Step 4- The Interview and Getting Paid

My conversion rate has been upwards of 80 percent. This is because I am selective of who I want to work with and people know that.

It's like hanging a sign outside that says 'Only grilled chicken served here." That kind of place will never attract people who don't like grilled chicken.

For those clients who I can't work with. I simply let them know why and recommend a product or service that can help them.

Tip: Don't be afraid to offer the products of an affiliate. Your prospect will appreciate it.

These are the interview questions. I usually spend 30 to 45 minutes helping them on the phone or via Skype or GoToMeeting.

1 Find out what his goals are and what he expects to get from this arrangement.

"What is your vision for this business? 12 months from this date and looking back. What would have needed to happen for you to be happy?"

After John tells me, I repeat his answers to him so he knows I'm paying attention.

2 Find out where his today and what is standing in his way.

"So you made $303 million last year and would like to be closer to $310 million 12 months from today.

How happy do you think your customers are with your business?

How many more customers would you like to have in the next 12 months?"

3 Now that you know where they are and where they want to be, fill in the gap by asking them questions that will lead them to feel they are building this plan with you.

I always build up-sells, back-end systems and help them setup sales sequences.

For example let's say Mary owns a high-end fashion brand. This is how the conversation may go.

Me- "Your main product is shoes. Is there anything else you feel your customers would like to have within 30 days of buying this shoe?"

Mary-"Yes. Many people like our $400 earrings. "

Me-"Do you think your clients would like that as a one click upsell? Do u think clients want your event as well at one click up-sell? What percentage of them do you think would buy?

Mary-" Yes that would be cool. About 20% of the 15,000 people who have bought the shoes would buy."

Me-"Is there anything else of value that you could give them somewhere in the next 12 months? Do people ask for a competitor's or a product that you don't sell?"

Mary-"We have a new $1,500 purse that we could show them."

Me-"Awesome. Do you think if we sent out a campaign via letter, email or brochure to all those who bought shoes if they'd like a discount on purse? What percentage of them do you think would purchase it?"

Mary-"That's an interesting idea. Yes. We could sell it for $1,400 to about 50% of them. "

Me-"By my calculation that means you could make $1.2 million with the earrings and $9.8 million with the purse campaign. That's $11 million more. Not too shabby huh?"

Mary-"You're right. That's a good plan."

Here is where you help her make money from her past customers
Me-"How many customers do you have over the last 2 years?"

Mary-"7,000"

Me- "Is there anything they want that you sell that they don't already own?"

Mary-"We used to sell a lot of jewelry sets for $700 but we haven't explored that option in a while."

Me-"If you offered that to your 7000 customers, what percentage of them do you think would like that?"

Mary-"At least 15% of them."

Me-"That could make you an extra $735,000"

I end with showing them how to build a list and some changes they could make to their websites and content strategy

Me- "You said you have 70,000 in your list. How are you growing that list?"

Mary-"Facebook ads, Google Ad words and some magazines"

Me-" Is there a reason you don't have Instagram and YouTube ads?"

Mary-"We have tried them but didn't see much conversion. Is there something we should know?"

Me-"Yes. Instagram is really just a TV screen in a customer's pocket. If done right, you could make a lot of money. Let's talk about your website's lead generation as well."

This is the part where I diagnose their lead generation systems both online and offline. We also talk about their product mix etc.

Prescribe and Close the path with numbers
Me-"Based on what you've told me it sounds like we could bring in over $11.7 million by doing what we have discussed. By creating the back-end systems, the up-sells, reactivation and creating better ads is that correct?"

"Does that sound like a good effective plan to you? Would you like me to help you implement the plan?"

Mary-"Definitely! When can we start?"

What happens next?
I sign them up for either my one day business growth session $50,000 or my monthly strategic coaching and growth program $10,000/m.

The client then can come over for a one on one Whiteboard session where I look at what they are currently doing, what needs to be fixed and what can be maximized. Clients appreciate this because a fresh pair of eyes can put things in perspective.

You will also notice that I have them come to me or we work via Skype or GoToMeeting for my monthly program. There are many reasons for this but one of the main ones is that it helps if the client is away from their business and in my office in California. It helps to clear their minds and they can think more strategically when they don't have to be putting out fires or answering emails at work.

Those were the simple steps that did it for me

I have just taken you through one of the best ways to grow your list and increase your revenue.

I have also showed you how I do it.

This will work for you if you are a Coach, Consultant and if run a Professional Services business.

Some examples of businesses this is great for are

- Accounting, Tax Preparation, Bookkeeping and Payroll Services
- Legal services, Financial Services, Real Estate leasing firms
- Healthcare Practices, Advertising/Marketing Agencies, Education and Consulting Firms and Infopreneurs

Would you like me to help you get the same results?

At sundry times I offer workshops and training sessions for coaches, consultants and entrepreneurs who are in the professional services industry.

Visit http://www.growingstartup.com/training

Automated Business Growth Systems That Turn Marketing into Profit

This is a real and proven system that will show you how to increase your sales, and show you how to automate your profit generation consistently.

This system does the following:

1. Generates leads consistently and turns them into recurring month on month profits
2. Increases your significance in your marketplace and spreads word of mouth without spending a fortune
3. Gives you more time to be creative in your business without working every single hour of the day.

You are reading here because you want greater freedom, contribution, significance and flexibility–with increased profits.

The 3 main ways to grow a business are

1. Increase the number of clients

2. Increase the amount of money each client pays per transaction

3. Increase the number of times a client comes back to buy from you. (Repeat customers)

Many businesses in your industry are concentrating on the number 1 and are probably struggling with getting it right.

NO need to fear or worry!!!

I will show you how to increase the size of transaction and get repeat customers systematically.

Before you contact me… let me know show you some simple strategies you can use to increase your sales, multiply repeat clients and increase word of mouth.

Strategy 1-Increase sales
A dentist was having a slow month and wanted to get more sales without spending too much.

He put out an Ad and offered teeth whitening, x-rays and a consultation for $150.

Here's the catch…his offer said "If you are not pleased with our service, we will refund the entire amount. No questions asked."

This dentist received so many leads, he was overwhelmed.

Why did this work?

It's called risk reversal.
In your business today, it is likely that you are putting all or most of the risk on the client.

When you pro-actively say that you will take the risk even before you offer exceptional service, it creates 3 thoughts in the client's mind.

Thought 1

This business must be very sure of their quality or they would not be offering such a deal.

Thought 2

This business must be one of integrity if they are willing to take the risk upfront.

The most important thought is,

" I should at least try them. I HAVE NOTHING TO LOSE."
You see how easy this is?

Here is another bonus strategy you can use today to INCREASE PROFITS AND MULTIPLY WORD OF MOUTH in your industry.

Strategy 2
We call this the Referral System because it is an automated and cheap way to grow a business
Let me teach you how to do it for free!
First,
Write down the names and phone numbers of 3 clients that you have served in the last 4 months.

These must be clients that you are sure will remember the excellent service you provided.

Here is the script you will use, assuming your business sells furniture.

"Hi Mary, my team and I wanted to reach out to you today because two months ago we sold you a set of high quality conference tables. We were talking about how pleasant it was to deal with you and we would love to do business with other clients of your caliber. Clients who appreciate exceptional service and quality products. Can you share the names of 2 to 3 business owners you know who would love to receive an offer from us? We promise to exceed their expectations as usual. Thank you and have a great day. "

Simple isn't it.

I personally have never been refused this simple request.

In fact, what is likely to happen is that the client will offer more referrals than you asked for.

Side note: You can also ask for an introduction. I have even seen business owners ask for the opportunity to present their offerings to another business' clients.

How to make this a system

The way to make this is a system is to automate it on a weekly or monthly basis.

If you are going to use the referral system, you can start by using the first Tuesday of the month to reach out to 50 to 100 clients as a test.

Track results to see how many of them convert and how much money you make.

11

A simple formula to make sure your foundation is right

First, the foundation:

As always, start with the client, user or customer in mind.

Step 1: Define the Market You Can Create the Most Value In

First, identify who you wants and is willing to pay for your product

Who is willing and able to pay for my product?

Is your ideal customer a female corporate banker who lives 30 miles away from her office? Is she actively looking for a way to automate her payroll? Is she frustrated with her bookkeeper?

Second, decide on what your message, positioning and differentiation will be.

This is about defining what you do, but also what sets you apart from other similar startups and demonstrates that you know that ideal user better than them.

Who are you to your user? The mobile ecommerce option? Are you the safer option? The cheapest? The one who delivers in 3 days?

Third, find a way to distribute your message and product.

Some businesses use social media to get their message to their customers. When you watch a video on YouTube or Netflix, the owner of the video used YouTube or your local TV network as their media distributor.

Other businesses use traditional retail outlets and physical media such as billboards, flyers and brochures. When you buy food using from Seamless or Postmates, the distribution channel could either be the Internet via an app, website or over the phone.

Some startups use physical media with QR codes or their websites printed on them.

The most profitable businesses are geniuses at using multiple distribution channels effectively.

What forms of distribution will give your customer easy access to your message and products?

Remember the process is always; market segmentation, positioning and distribution respectively.

Step 2: Grow the Startup with Strategy
If you increase the number of users, the number of things that each of them buys, and get them to make purchases more often, your growth will be exponential.

The below equations demonstrate this:

Let's set the following values:

Price of product: $100
Number of customers: 100
Number of times each user pays you in a year: 1

$100 per product x 100 users x 1 = $10,000 per year.

Now let's increase the price and customers by just 20%, and turn a single-purchase customer into one who buys something twice a year: each of them.

$120 per product x 120 users x 2 purchases per year = $28,800 a year.

Notice how your revenue more than doubled in a year.

Let's assume you are ambitious and you find a way to raise every value.

$300 per product x 30,000 users x 2 purchases per year = $18,000,000

Do you see how quickly you got to a million dollars?

Do this calculation using your business as an example.

Step 3: Get New Customers and Increase Revenue Using These Tactics

First, Risk Reversal Offers. We have found out that businesses that use Freemium, free trials or use-before-you-buy models usually get a lot of early traction.

Secondly, our research has shown that customers buy more from businesses that they feel they know a lot about.

The lesson here is to educate the customer on what the benefits of your product or service are. Unfortunately too many businesses talk more about when they were established and how many branches they have instead of educating their prospects.

8 Ways to Increase Revenue Growth

1 Increasing revenue by increasing your prices

Many founders are afraid of increasing their prices just because they don't know if it will work.

Think about it.

Do you think Steve Jobs asked for public permission before releasing the IPhone at $499?

Today you can get an IPhone 7 at $649 and even $769.

You can A/B test to find out which price point works best for the value you are providing.

2 Increase your conversion rate

The word every founder loves to talk about is traffic.

Many do not realize that you can have 1 million unique visitors or downloads and still be broke.

What many founders forget is that many of the news articles they read are not writing by entrepreneurs

What is more important than likes and shares is actual conversions or sales.

You can increase your conversion rate by educating your users more on the benefits of using your product.

You can demonstrate the benefits (not the features)

Tweak your opt-in pages, landing pages and copy to see what people respond to.

Test, Test Test.

3 Get more targeted leads

People say the more leads you get the better.

That is a BIG lie.

The more targeted your leads are, the better.

In my experience, most founders can't even tell you who their ideal user is. The trap is wanting everyone to download your app and only getting 3% conversion.

Many startups have gotten funded, been featured in TechCrunch and still failed.

If you have to pay more for a high quality lead, DO IT.

4 Change your business model

Just because you have an app, a website or a hardware product does not mean you have to copy the same business model as everyone else.

Part of the reason Dell become a billion dollar business and Tesla is making waves is because they both did not choose the conventional business models.

Consider subscription, Advertising, into-products, events, affiliate offers and consulting as supplementary or complementary to your current model.

5 Sell more stuff

One way to grow your startup is to sell more stuff to your users.

You can either sell a premium package or just add more high value features and charge for them.

Facebook has become increasingly useful because businesses find more ways to use the service to reach their audience.

Keep in mind however that people pay for results so don't just create features for the sake of it.

6 Offer Value Added Affiliate Options

Depending on where you live, when you buy a house, you get offered deals for a gardener, swimming pool, insurance and other value added services.

This will work for almost any industry.

If your startup offers project management software, your users may also require a CRM, Email Auto-Responder or Payroll Management services.

Contact other startups and create a profit share agreement where you offer each other's services to your users.

7 Set up recurring payments, subscriptions and membership packages.

Sass and Media startups have found this a great way to grow their revenue.

Is there a premium package you can provide for a fixed fee every month?

8 Attract Sponsorship and Advertising

There is definitely a sponsor or business that would like to have access to your list of users.

You can set up a joint venture partnership with sponsors in exchange for money, traffic or other resources.

Consider business models such as reselling and licensing as well.

Conclusion

Probably the most overlooked way to grow a startup is through content.

Think about it. The more people know about a business, the more confident they are as to whether to buy or not.

Having blogs, videos and an effective content marketing strategy is necessary.

Even more important than that is to automate the entire process so you don't have to work all the time to make money.

13
Product Launch Case Study

Peter is the owner of Auto Genius Car dealership and needs cash to become profitable in a short time.

First Peter decides to offer a promotion for the next 10 days to attract new buyers.
The offer is "As long you qualify, you can buy any car at Auto Genius and drive it for 10 days. If after 10 days you feel you would like another vehicle or would want to upgrade, we will do that for you.
If after 10 days you feel this is not the time for you to buy a new car, you are free to return it in the same state with no defects and we will give you a full money back guarantee."

The second thing Peter setup was a referral system.
He took down the names, phone numbers and email addresses of every new customer.
He called them 5 days later and asked them to give him the contact details of someone they knew who would love to hear about the promotion but hadn't gotten the opportunity to come by the dealership. "

Peter's competitors laughed at him and said it would never work.
They said people would just buy the cars and return them just for fun.
They said no one would believe the promotion was real.

What do you think were the results of this campaign?

Auto Genius' sales went up 15 percent in 7 days.
To his surprise, only 5 percent of the people who bought the cars asked for their money back.
The other 95 percent either kept their cars or returned them and got an upgrade which meant even more money for Auto Genius
The great part is that the customers he contacted gave him an average of two referrals each.

That means he is on his way to doubling his revenue this year just from word of mouth.

Influence and Persuasion as Marketing Magnets

This section is a primer on some basic human psychological triggers. This does not describe every human being but understanding what motivates many people will help you do better.

What do most people want?
1 Results with little or no work
2 To be told what to do
3 Convenience, Speed and Ease

Human behavior to be conscious of
1 Its emotionally unacceptable for many (not all) people to blame themselves. It's usually someone or something else's fault like the government, their past, their employees, their industry or that no one else does things this way.

2 A lot of people are unintentionally selfish and always looking out for benefits and self-preservation. E.g. First thought is what's in it for me

3 Fear makes some people care too much about what others think of them. Many would act differently if they could be themselves or do something without anyone ever finding out. It's partly the reason why bold entrepreneur succeed without adding any extra skill. E.g. Celebs and all high profile scandals either lie to deceive or to save face, investors have fear of missing out

4 It's difficult for most of us to go somewhere they haven't seen themselves go or someone else.

5 Driven by insufficiency. E.g. the "I've got to have that to be complete syndrome" that makes people buy things they don't need and compare themselves to people they see online or in the media.

1 The power of instant gratification

Car dealerships offer test drives because they have found out that after driving a new car, the mind gets a taste of what we call Instant Gratification. The prospect gets to enjoy what it's like to drive a brand new car without paying for it. This rush of instant gratification plants a seed that is difficult for many people to uproot. After that test drive, people say their current vehicle starts to look and feel old. In many cases they return to trade in their old car or buy a new one.

The quicker you can get someone to experience your product, the easier it will be to persuade them to buy.
I heard of a piano salesman who would come and give his prospects a piano to keep in the home for about a week. By the time he returned to collect it, most of the homes decided to keep the piano and pay for it.

This happened because they had already gotten a taste of what it felt like to have a piano in the home. Their children were already enjoying the piano and were even considering getting lessons. All this instant gratification made it easy for the salesman to close the sale.
If his customers hadn't gotten to experience it beforehand, it would have been a tougher sell.

Free samples, free trials, free consultations, demonstrations and other try-before-you-buy tactics work very well.

What can you give people that will get them to experience the benefits of your product immediately?

2 People want results with little or no work on their part

Would you rather take cooking lessons from a top chef or would you rather have him make the food for you?
For most people they would rather have the food instead of the lessons.
You have heard it said that give a man a fish and you feed him for a day; teach a man to fish and you feed him for a lifetime.
Unfortunately that saying doesn't work for most businesses.

More often than not, your clients would rather have you do the work for them than to do it themselves.
The better you get at giving the client what they want without them doing any work, the more appealing your products will be.

People want things to be done for them. The less brain power they use, the better.
The path of least resistance is usually the most appealing so do well to add that to your marketing and product development.

The purpose of reading is not to flip pages.
The purpose of reading is to acquire knowledge.
This is why most people would rather watch TV than read a book.
It's not that they are dumb or lazy but that watching pre-packaged information is more appealing than digging for it yourself.

Whenever you get the chance, always say you will do the work for the customer or at least you will do most of it.
Offer to deliver instead of having the customer pick it up.
Offer to install instead of having the customer do it themselves.
Offer the research instead of giving them the sources of information.
You will notice this course comes with blueprints and systems that I have already created for you.

What Done-for-you products or services do you provide?
1
2
2

3 Direction provides certainty
Have you ever seen any advertisement or promotion that offers promises like these "3 easy steps to a better golf swing", "7 ways to become a better manager", "3 simple negotiation techniques for salespeople"?

Mobile Application developers have found out that by reducing the number of times someone has to tap their screens to get a certain result, the higher the engagement and user retention.

The reason these are so successful is because people will pay for certainty.
The more uncertain someone is about what your product will do for them, the less inclined they will be to buy.

As humans we have a fascination with maps, blueprints, formulas, tips and advice.
We will do almost anything to clear up doubt from our minds.
When someone tells you something you don't believe, you either go online to find the answer or ask someone else's opinion.

Successful companies know that their websites, retail space and sales materials should offer step by step instructions.
The mind will always seek the clearer option because it doesn't want to be in darkness.

Offer step by step instructions to your prospects.
People should know what to do if they want to buy something, speak to someone, try your product or have it delivered.
The simpler it is to find the BUY button, the more sales you will make.

Give them formulas, tips and steps to success.
No one ever bought anything and said "I bought this because it was so difficult to use".
Everyone brags about things that are easy to use.

Practice: 3 steps to ...

4 Give and people will feel compelled to give back
Jesus said "Give and it will be given back to you" Luke 6:38
This is a cardinal rule of life that works in the business world as well.

The more you do for someone, the more compelled they are to reciprocate.
Most people only discard things that they don't think are of a lot of value to them.

When someone buys you dinner or gives you a ride home or does you a favor, you feel obligated to return the favor.

Employees who don't contribute a lot are fired.
Politicians we feel aren't giving us what we want are not re-elected.
Even children go to the parent who will love them more and stay away from the one they fear.

Make it obvious to your customers what you are giving them and then give them more value than anyone else.
In my consulting business, I make sure that no client will ever be able to say they didn't get more than they paid for.
I always have bonuses and extra value that they didn't know they were going to receive.

The mistake some business owners make is that they don't let their clients know what they did for them.
Don't assume your value is obvious.
Repeat it over and over again.

What am I giving my ideal customer?
1
2
3

5 Use Authority in a field as leverage and those who don't have it will come to you

An old friend who wasn't very wealthy gave me a book but I didn't read it.
Three years later, it was recommended to me by a millionaire.
I read it in a day.

What happened was that I didn't think my friend was an authority on the subject so his recommendation wasn't very meaningful to me.

Husbands do it all the time.
They'll take advice from someone at work when their wife probably told them the same thing weeks before.

Business owners find that when a consultant speaks to their staff, it holds more water.
In many cases a consultant is called in just to say what the boss has been trying to tell his team for months.
The staff will do what the consultant says because they see her as an authority.

When people perceive that a lot of work went into making a decision, they believe the decision must be good.

It's the same with products.
Beauty products that claim they were made by 6 Swedish chemists' working day and night in a lab in Switzerland outsell those made by a generic brand made in Kentucky.

Always use authority as leverage.
If your product takes 8 hours to make, say it.
If you only use fresh ingredients say it. Even if all your competitors are doing the same.
If your head of Finance has a PHD, say it.
The more authority you can boast about, the more appealing your products will be to consumers.

What are some ways you can use this?
1
2
3

4 Use endorsements and you will inherit that other person's leverage

A young entrepreneur asked a billionaire to do a deal with him.
The billionaire was hesitant because it wasn't worth his time.

He wanted to help the young entrepreneur so he came up with a plan.

He said "I won't give you the money but I will walk with you publicly for a day in the presence of people who you want to do business with. After that day, everyone you want to deal with will be willing to do business with you."

As the story goes, after people say that the young entrepreneur was rubbing shoulders with a billionaire, they started reaching out to him for business deals.

That's the kind of leverage a good endorsement will give you.

The mistake many people make is that they seek the wrong kind of leverage.
They either do not know what kind of endorsement will impress their market or they overestimate the power of endorser.

For months I kept getting new clients because I had done business with a restaurant owner that they respected.

I knew celebrity endorsements worked but I was yet to find out that nearly any well placed endorsement works as well depending on the audience.
For example a client once told me that what made it easy for her to hire me was because she found out I had taken a certain course at a particular school she admired.

I didn't even think it was important to mention that I had been to that school but for this client, it meant everything.

Great entrepreneurs learn to use whatever they find to increase their appeal.
Instead of building a following, you can skillfully get a personality or an organization.

Big brands will wait till an influencer has millions of followers and then they will create a capsule collection to exploit that following.

Nike makes billions of dollars from using the celebrity endorsements of athletes.
Many people would rather hire a Harvard educated senior manager than a manager who attended a community college.

It does not necessarily mean the Harvard graduate is better but the school's name carries leverage.

Entrepreneurs who sell to other businesses make sure they mention who their former clients are.

If you have it, use it skillfully.

Three sources of endorsements
1
2
3

5 Words and images that show an individual amplified consistently are greater than what they think of themselves

The body usually will not go where the mind cannot see.

What skilled marketers do is to find out what their prospects can relate with and then they exaggerate that image to influence them.

For example, you know you won't look exactly like that model wearing those clothes in the commercial but you buy the clothes anyway.

If the model in the picture was ten years younger than you, there is a chance that you would not have bought the outfit.

The model chosen was what you could relate with.
The model's beautiful figure is likely an exaggeration of what you look like right now.

Those two things are like pulling levers in someone's mind.

We see this in the film industry and music industry.
People who watch something long enough will start to mimic what they see.
Some people start walking, talking and even changing the way they live to match what they see.

For business owners, always make sure to portray images that are exaggerated and embellished versions of your prospects.
When you want to influence a CEO, paint a picture of her running a more profitable business because she is using your products.

Failure to show an embellished picture of your prospect is a mistake.

How does my customer see himself/herself?

What would be a good embellished and exaggerated image of him/her?

6 Once I was blind now I can see

In John 9, a man is blind and gets healed by Jesus. Verse 32 and 33 offer sentences that every business owner should emulate.
The people said "Never before has anyone heard of opening the eyes of a man born blind. If this man were not from God, He could not do anything like this. "
Jesus could have argued that He was the Son of God but it would have been difficult to convince people.
The results spoke louder than words.

Kenneth E. Hagin called that the "Dinner bell effect".

Nothing influences people better than results.

Fitness instructors will tell you that the more before and after photos they show, the faster their business grows.
Pastors will tell you that the more testimonies of healings they advertise, the more members they receive.
If you can show what someone's life or business will be after they use your product, it's like making the decision for them.

When you see someone just like you doing what you desire, you tell yourself "If they did it, I can do that too."

Some examples of pitches you can use-

My product will take you from…..
Sadness to happiness
Fat to skinny
Lack to abundance
Darkness to light
Blindness to sight
Debt to profits
Complex to simple
Ugly to beautiful
Plain to stylish
Small results to major gains

You should craft a message that says "Before us, you could only have this but with us you can have that".

Before ……………………… you could only have(do, experience)…………………….but with ………………………….. You can have …………………..

8 People buy for emotional and logical reasons

Some of the first courses I ever sold were to people who had jobs but wanted to start a business.
My research showed that my ideal customer (let's call him Sam) was a male between the ages of 30 to 42.
Sam had at least 7 years of work experience, was married with kids and made somewhere between $30,000 to $48,000 a year.
He was tired of living someone else's dream and wished he could contribute more.
Sam also wanted flexibility and freedom.
Lastly, he wanted to make enough money so he could quit his job and live a more fulfilling life.

I deduced that Sam's greatest desires are
1 Freedom
2 Wealth
3 Contribution

Freedom to do whatever he wanted.

Wealth so he could live in comfort without having to worry about money.
Contribution so that he could turn his ideas into profits and to be appreciated by people around him.

If you take a closer look, out of the three desires, only one of them had to do with material things.
His other two drivers were emotional.

This is the same with your prospects.
They may want food as their physical desire but their emotional desire is satisfaction.
They may want a ride as their physical desire for transportation but their emotional desire may be to save time or to impress their neighbors.
If you are selling a house, make sure you know if they are looking for a home big enough for their children or if they want one just to have a place to stay.

Smart business owners know how to use the physical desire as the bait and the emotional desire as their back up.

There is a marketing proverb that says "People don't buy because they understand you. They buy because they feel understood."

My customer's emotional desires-

My customer's physical desires-

9 Stories create word of mouth and increase sales

News media has stayed relevant for centuries because we love to hear stories.
The entrepreneur who started from the bottom, worked his way out of poverty, faced ridicule and is now a hugely successful is a story we all love to hear.

The rags to riches or lack to profits or idea to success story works very well.

It definitely beats hearing about a plain product in a box.

The better you are at telling stories, the easier people will be able to talk about your business.
The more people repeat your story, the more respected you will be in your marketplace.

What's your story?
Is it on your website?
Do your customers know it?

15

Psychological Triggers That Attract, Inspire and Motivate People

If a brand can impress you, it will be easy for them to control your buying decision.

No one likes to hear that.

We genuinely like to think that we make all decisions rationally without any external influence.

People will do on the outside whatever they see themselves doing on the inside

You have to understand that self-interest is the core of trigger of every human being.

Even when many of us do selfless things, they do it because it makes us feel good.

That feeling of helping someone is enough of a drug to keep us doing more.

What separates us is those who do good with a good motive and those who do good with a bad one. I pray we never join the latter group.

1 A confident person can bend less confident people to his will.

Many times it's not even the best employee who gets the raise or the more qualified politician who gets the vote. Confidence is usually enough to influence someone.

2 Stories of exploits make a person more attractive.

The athlete who wins the Olympics. The army general who captured the enemy with only 300 men. The immigrant who moved to New York with nothing and became a billionaire. The mother who raised 4 sons on her own while running a business. The math genius who got into college at age 12.

If you have stories of exploits, use them as your flag and people will seek you out.

3 Free trials

People are more likely to buy if they have tried a product and found it satisfactory.

4 Reciprocity

When someone gives you a lot, it stirs up obligation and makes you want to return the favor. I don't recommend intentionally obligating people to you because that is unethical manipulation. Be good to people and most times they'll return the favor.

5 Celebrity is a magnet

I'm not sure why this works exactly but people who are thought of as important or celebrities wield a lot of influence. I reckon it's our attraction of people who have more attention than we do. I've seen examples of people who are unknown but respected just because someone called them a celebrity.

6 Social Proof aka everyone is doing it

Restaurants that have a line outside attract more customers. It is no indication that the food is good but as long as there is a queue outside, people assume it is good.

7 I don't want to look bad or it will make me look good in their eyes

Research says people post content that has a headline that will make them look smart before their peers.

Some experts say that people would pay more to prevent embarrassment than they would to get fame.

My brother Vijay jokes that many men would even fight just to prevent embarrassment.

8 The allure of satisfaction is a strong one

If a friend tells you that a certain activity gave them a lot of fulfillment and satisfaction, you would probably want to know more.

9 Grace –to be loved unconditionally

People are drawn to friends who don't judge them. When we feel that we can do no wrong in someone's eyes, it gives us motivation to do better.

10 Sense of achievement

A study was done where employees were given bonuses every quarter of the year without their consent.

The management found out that morale was higher when employees felt that they had deserved the bonuses.

Businesses with salespeople usually have a leaderboard for this same reason.

People are motivated when they have a goal to aim for.

The sense of achievement increases when they have competition and when there is some form of award or public gesture to show that they won.

11 Gamification works

Imagine if on the first day of college you were told that there would be no mid semester or final exams. What if you were told that there would be no vacations. You would stop and start anytime you felt like it.

Many students would never be able to stay for more than 6 months without dropping out.

Its human nature to want steps, paragraphs, events, schedules and some form of order.

Whenever you have something that is too long or difficult for your client to consume, break it down into little chunks.

Part of the reason a lot of people don't finish books they start is because going through 300 pages without the right breaks feels like a chore.

12 A quick and easy fix

The words quick and easy will forever be useful in communication.

I don't think anyone is attracted to delays and hardship.

13 No consequences and Risk free

One of the strategies I have taught you is to present offers that take the risk away from the transaction.

It's human nature to always be cautious of whether there will be penalties or consequences.

The less penalties, the more attractive the offer.

14 Something for nothing

The restaurant that offers a free sandwich just because it's a national holiday can use that as a lead magnet to drive sales.

15 Bonuses and more than you paid for

Whenever you offer a bonus, it creates an extra incentive to want to buy from you.

16 Association and comparison

Things people associate with your product will either motivate them to buy or stay away from you.

One reason fitness centers and gyms struggle to keep their doors open is because most of the population associates keeping fit with hard work and sweat.

Gyms that realize that looking good is a better motivation usually do better.

17 Scarcity and our love for rare things

Whenever there is more supply than demand, a product becomes a commodity.

An effective strategy is to offer a limited trial or offer limited quantities of a product.

18 Authority

People will be most persuaded by you when they see you as having knowledge and credibility on the topic.

19 Commitment

Commitment; especially publicly makes it difficult for people to turn down an offer or to stop using a product.

Many of us will find it difficult to switch our email providers just because of all the email we have amassed over the years.

In technology, the more photos or content a user uploads, the more likely they are to stick around.

20 Testimonials

The "once I was blind but now I can see" strategy works well.

Whether it's restored furniture, weight loss testimonials or a co-worker who takes a course and gets a higher salary. It's almost impossible to resist a testimonial that shows the before and after results.

Hiring and Culture

A company is a collection of people who are working (or are supposed to be) working towards a common goal.

The businesses that have lasted for decades have had exceptional management and culture.

The reason great culture is difficult for so many founders to get right is because of how they think.

Your business is a direct reflection of your mindset.

Management is driven by love and empathy.

Love is all about giving. There is no selfishness in love.

If you love someone, and know they will be better off working for a competitor, do not hire them.

It would surprise you how many people just hire someone so their competitor can't have them.

If you love someone, you will give them the right hours and right compensation.

Another thing to note about culture is that you can engineer it.

People who think they can't are either ignorant or dishonest.

The culture will inevitably be driven by the founder's values either intentionally or unintentionally.

Amos 3:3 says Can two walk together, except they be agreed?

In hiring you have to decide what kind of skills you need to get to your desired goal as a business.

Secondly you have to decide on what kind of behavior, vision and values are acceptable to you.

Your business is your responsibility so don't let the world tell you how to run it.

If you hire people who you don't enjoy being around, you will ultimately regret it no matter how smart they are.

Sometime ago I was in dire need of a developer.

I found one of the best developers and he was even willing to work for less than he usually did.

What bothered me was that his social media posts were full of cynicism and consistent criticizing of preachers.

For someone, that may have not been a big deal but I personally don't keep company with vulgar people.

If I decided to work with him, I would have had to pretend to be okay with his behavior.

Instead of hiring and then trying to change him, I abandoned the project and tabled it for later.

Hire people who share the same goals and drive as you do.

They don't have to be copycats of you otherwise all you'll have is a group of yes-men who won't bring fresh ideas to the table.

Hire people who you respect and can trust to do what's right whether you are watching over them or not.

Hire people you can train to become better than they are today.

In addition to this, ALWAYS check references and ask important questions.

It would surprise you how many people never check references.

The responsible thing to do is call the references and ask why they think the person is a good hire.

Find out what makes them unique and prod till you are convinced they are a good fit.

For more senior roles, make sure you spend a lot of time with the person before you hire them.

Reid Hoffman said he spent at least 40 hours with Jeff Weiner before he was certain he was the best person for the CEO role.

To get the best people, try to get introductions from people you already know are good at what they do.

This is because the best people usually have friends or know people who are just like them.

There is a company in Silicon Valley that has an interesting approach to this.

After hiring a new team member, they ask them, "Give us a list of names of people who are as competent as you are?"

This way they are able to get a list of potential hires that fit their criteria.

This is important.

If your business is small and half of your team does not have the same mindset, it will feel like you are running half of a business.

One of my clients was always complaining about his staff.

I told him, "Either fire them or train them. If they don't conform to your training, look for new people."

Firing isn't fun or easy but sometimes it's necessary.

An entrepreneur paid for advertising but his team kept telling him that only one or two leads were coming in on a daily basis.

He later found out that hundreds of calls had come in but his staff had been unable to convert them into customers.

To hide their incompetence, they blamed the campaign.

After firing them and hiring new people, he saw that for every dollar he spent, he got over nine dollars back.

How to fire

I've been fired twice.

Once was because I started freelancing during my internship that my boss felt was going to be competition for him.

He called me into the conference room at 10 am and said "I'd like us to divorce our working relationship but stay friends."

He gave me 2 weeks' severance and I left that day.

What made me unhappy was that I had planned to leave 3 months prior but I felt the business needed me so I stayed.

We are still acquainted today and I have consulted with him on a couple of projects.

The second time I was fired, it was a quasi-partnership.

The CEO and I disagreed on the business model and the customer segment to focus on.

He sent me an email to say he had spoken to his father about it and decided that we couldn't work together anymore.

This time no severance followed. Lol.

Looking back, I respect both of them for doing what they felt was right.

The latter encounter should have happened in person and with severance.

If you are going to fire someone, be considerate.

If you can write a recommendation letter or introduce them to a better opportunity, please do it.

If you suspect someone has to be let go, speak with them about their performance and give them the opportunity to change.

If that doesn't work out, they will know that they "fired" themselves.

In closing, culture works best when people can see an example.

I know of a CEO who preached good values to his team and was later found to be gambling on a Monday afternoon at a casino. His team never took him seriously after that.

You can't tell your team not to talk behind each other's backs and then turn around and gossip.

If you show them that you trust them, they'll be a reflection of that trust.

If you are not seen as a productive leader, the team will gravitate to the manager who seems to be the most productive one.

Follow these guidelines and you will build a strong culture based on love, vision and execution.

P.S

One way to evaluate if a present employee is a good fit is to use these questions.

1 What did you do today?

2 What results did you get?

3 What problems and challenges did you face?

If the person keeps giving you the wrong answers to these after a while, you can let them go.

Secondly, I personally don't advise that you should hire people who have too many side businesses.

An entrepreneur is likely to leave you immediately they start making more money with their side gig.

If you want to hire an entrepreneur, you can employ her as a contractor or keep it in the back of your mind that they are not with you for the long term.

17
Business don't sign checks. Humans do.

All checks are signed by or approved by a human being.
Having this mindset will help you use these strategies effectively and not be afraid to pitch a corporation. In fact, a corporation is just a group of humans.

This is how I stack up the mental magnets that cause people to attend my events.
It is also effective for influencing someone who is stubborn.

Step 1 Offer word of mouth testimonials from friends or colleagues who are your past clients or know about you.

Step 2 Show social proof in the form of other respected people using your product.

Step 3 Demonstration of achievements such as stories of exploits.

Step 4 Showing the brand's worth. If your business is worth billions, be sure to mention it. If you have respected clients, talk about them. If your product development process is unique, flaunt it.
In the cosmetics industry, they found that people are impressed by products that are made by European laboratories.
For some reason a new anti-aging lotion that was invented in Kentucky doesn't have the same sizzle as the one made in the mountains of Switzerland.

Step 5 Crowd herd effect of mentioning how many clients you have or how many people will be attending your event.

6 Continuity promise of continuous support in the future. If it's an event, include a promise of future trainings. If it's a B2B sales pitch, offer ongoing support.

7 Risk reversal of full refund after first day of event or offer money back guarantee or free returns.

8 Show the differentiation of benefits.

This could be customization or a comparison to a lesser benefit offered by competitors.

9 Communicate the logical justification.
Many people either have to discuss a buying decision with their spouse, lawyer or accountant. Give them the words so they don't say the wrong thing.

10 Borrowed celebrity
If you have any famous clients, speakers or associations, use them. I've heard of a business that won a deal because one of those who pitched was wearing a tie from his alma mater. It just so happened that one of the decision makers had attended the same school over a decade before.

How to Write Magnetic Sales Letters

This is the structure you should follow. No gimmicks included.

You tell the reader:
1 Here is what I've got for you (the product)
2 Here is what it'll do for you (the benefit)
3 Here is what you should do next (call to action)

The only caveat here is to answer all the questions that the reader may have about you or your product.
This is a reminder to understand what your customer wants before you write a sales letter.

The verbose versions of this are as follows-

How to Create a Moneymaking Webinar
1 Show the problem
2 Support what you said with research, reports or some other kind of third party data
3 Magnify the problem
4 Offer your solution
5 Tell them what to do to get the solution

20
The Loaded Presentation Variation

1 Headline communicates who the prospect will become after using your product
2 Establish Authority by speaking of your experience and results
3 State what they are doing wrong and why it doesn't work
4 Show them what works and why it works
5 Offer free help that will cause immediate change
6 Affirm and remind them that it will work for them as well
7 Use mental triggers such as endorsements, bonuses, scarcity, social proof,
8 State call to action

How to Create Videos That Make Money

Purpose of the video could be to sell or presell/affiliate offer or get leads or awareness or anticipation for a launch/promotion.

1 Start with asking a question the audience can relate to
"Are you overwhelmed with having too much to do at work?
Are you looking for a simple way to file your taxes?
Do you feel like you are paying too much for electricity?"

2 Take away their doubts and objections by giving them answers

3 Show them the benefits and repeating the desired outcome
4 Offer your solution as an authority
5 Show them a good self-serving reason for them to take immediate action
6 Activate the mental triggers such as bonuses, social proof and risk reversal
7 Tell them what to do next

The Reality of the limitless life

I saved the best for last.

The advantage we have as Christians is that we have the wisdom, ability, wealth and grace of God working with us.

We literally have the Person who knows more about business and success than anyone else who ever lived guiding us daily.

The reason many believers have not been successful in business is because they don't know we have an advantage.

Most of the teachings on faith in business are about ethics and morality.

Those are a part of our nature as children of God but it's not ethics you need to grow a business.

Wisdom from God is what builds empires.

What's more impressive? Being able to outrun men in an Olympic contest or being able to outrun the fastest horses for miles.

- What's more remarkable? Being able to deliver vaccines to one thousand sick people or speaking words in a crusade and 1000 people receiving healing instantly?
- Would you prefer to buy truckloads of food for the hungry or to be able to feed over 10,000 men, women and children in mere minutes without spending money?

Do you see where I'm going with this?

I'm comparing the natural human feats we see celebrated today with examples of what divine ability can do.

As children of God we have abilities that are largely untapped.

2 chronicles 9:22–23 says Solomon was richer and wiser than all (not some) the kings of the earth. All (not some) sought his presence to hear him speak.

- This means there wasn't a king on earth who had more wealth or problem solving ability than Solomon did.
- There wasn't an expense he couldn't pay for or a problem that was outside his scope of ability.
- Whether you wanted to know the best way to build a ship, plan a city or cure a diseases, Solomon could tell you exactly how to do that.

How?

Divine ability

How do we use this limitless ability?

By acting on the Word and daring the impossible.

Jesus Christ told us that we are now greater than Solomon.

He also told us that we would do even greater things than He did.

We have seen modern day examples of miraculous feats by believers but not enough because as a family, we have been taught to think like natural men.

We have accepted their limits and talked, acted and lived like them.

2 Peter 1:4 says we have the nature of God now.

What does that mean?

Let's compare the nature of a Toyota Corolla to the nature of a Hennessey Venom Gt or a Bugatti Veyron Super Sport. No one would even bother racing a regular sedan with a sports car because the abilities would be unmatched.

That's what happened to us after we received Zoe (the life and nature of God). It was like putting the engine of a sports car into the shell of a sedan. Before we may have been able to get from 0 to 100 in 60 seconds but now we can do the same in a mere 3 seconds.

It would be nice to be the fastest athlete in the world but we have something better.

We have the divine ability to get results in record time.

- It may take others months to receive their first 1 million customers but it can happen for you in a day.
- It may take decades for others to see $100 billion in profits but it can happen for you in a day.
- Imagine starting a business today and having 90% market share in 30 days. Can you do that?
- Imagine coming up with a cure that can wipe out a killer disease in a week. Is that beyond the ability of God in you?

Many quote Philippians 4:13 and say they can do all things through Christ's ability but they don't believe what I just said.

You know why?

They want to see an example first. They forget that the Bible says we don't walk by what we see but purely by faith in the Word of God.

Why quote the scripture that says all things are possible to the believer and yet deny your ability to do the impossible?

How do we use this limitless ability?

By acting on the Word and daring the impossible.

The reason many Christians haven't seen spectacular feats in their lives is because they listen to people who aren't familiar with the limitless ability of Jesus Christ.

While some believe they can receive complete healing today by faith, others believe it will take a year.

It's really as simple as hearing words of faith and acting on them.

I had the ability to lay hands on a sick person and have them healed for years but until I heard Pastor Chris Oyakhilome and Kenneth E Hagin explain it, I lived in darkness.

I had the name and authority of Jesus to cause whatever changes I wanted in my life but until I read E.W Kenyon's books I just lived like everyone else.

Let's hear and act on the Word.

The trick of the devil is to make you think you lack some ability, revelation or sufficiency.

The Bible says we are complete in Christ and that He's our sufficiency.

Welcome to the limitless life. There is nothing outside the realm of your ability in Christ.

Extras-

The mind will usually pick whatever action is easy to do.

Don't let that happen by default.

Many entrepreneurs are caught up in learning, reading, attending conferences and watching videos without implementing what they studied.

People buy courses and books that will just end up on their shelf.

In the words of E.W Kenyon,

"Make your brain work. It will sweat, but make it work. It will improve. It will develop until you become a wonder to those around you."

I'd like to add that you should also make your hands work. Analysis without action produces no results.

Epilogue

Thank you for taking the time to work on your business.

What you have received from this book makes you part of the few marketing masters in your city or nation.

Finally here are 5 things you can change in your business today to make you a better entrepreneur.

1. By changing who you sell to and targeting higher value clients, you can multiply your income this month.
2. By changing the sources of your leads you can increase sales.
3. By increasing prices by 20 percent, you can increase profits
4. By creating new products or positioning your current ones differently you can become more valuable and attractive.
5. By creating a follow up sequence, you can deliver more value and get more sales.

Bonus Campaign

When you visit http://www.growingstartup.com/free you will see a free campaign that has made millions of dollars in sales. This is my gift to you. Use it liberally and let me know your results.

The following pages are bonuses that will add to the value you have already received.

They are culled from speeches and blog posts I have shared over the years.

You are also invited to our events and workshops which may be in a city near you. Visit http://www.growingstartup.com/training to find out.

Your life and business are blessed.

Jeffrey A. Manu

Bonus content-

The best kind of customer

At each of our workshops and seminars, I ask the new business owners how many of them own a Marketing book that wasn't written by me.

Predictably everyone who is interested in Marketing has books by other authors.

If you like pizza, it's very likely that you have ordered from more than two or three places in the last 6 months.

This proves that the best kind of customer is someone who has proof of a recent purchase.

The best kind of customer is someone who has already bought from your competitor in the past.

This kind of customer is already motivated to buy again because they know what kind of product you are selling.

1 The 3 Fastest Ways to Attract High Paying and High Quality Leads

These are 3 of the fastest ways to more than quadruple your traffic in the shortest time possible.

- Leveraged relationships such as joint ventures, affiliates and partnerships
- Leveraged appearances
- Leveraged Advertising

The whole point of leverage is to do the activity that brings the greatest results.

It will take you about 43 hours to drive from New York to San Francisco.

You could also fly the same journey in just 6 hours.

This analogy is important because the point of travelling is to get to your destination. Not to spend hours in a vehicle.

Your business is the same. You can either try a bunch of tactics to drive people to your site or office but wouldn't you rather do a few things that will deliver the same result?

A lot of business owners are busy doing things that contributed little or nothing to their business growth.

The whole point of a strategy or tactic is the result. Not the activity itself.

Leveraged relationships-Joint Ventures, Partnerships and Affiliates

As the apocryphal story goes, a young man visited a billionaire asking for his help.

Young man- "I would like you to help me get access to the top investors in this city. You will receive half of my company in return. "

Billionaire- "There is a faster way. Tomorrow you will walk side by side with me at the center of the city square. Many of the top investors will see that we are acquainted.

After that, everyone will want to do business with you. "

True to his word, the billionaire's public endorsement of the young man was enough leverage to make other feel it was okay to do business with him.

There are people, businesses and organizations who already have the ears, eyes, wallets and contact details of your prospects.

We call such people hosts. It is analogous with the host/parasite relationships in nature.

What you need to do is to find them and come into a partnership with them where they give you access to their list in exchange for something mutually beneficial.

Celebrity endorsements work the same way.

In my experience, the best form of this kind of leverage is when the host acts as a reseller or distributor.

You want the host or partner to treat your product or service as a valuable add-on.

Look for partners who can use your product as a cross sell or upsell.

The way to do this is to identify what products your customers buy before, with or after they purchase your product.

When I sold shoes, we identified others who were already selling to our prospects. People who sold shirts, ties, belts and suits were all worthy candidates for leveraged relationships.

This was great because every time they sold a suit, they would pitch our shoes as a complementary product.

We made money every time they did.

This arrangement lavishly transfers the trust that the host has spent millions of dollars to accrue unto your brand.

This is why so many authors add that they have a New York Times bestseller. They know that all it takes is selling a few thousand copies in your first week and then you can claim that title. Nobody bothers to check how many you sold in latter weeks.

Case study

One of my clients runs a car garage. Their services include fixing cars and giving them new paint jobs.
He makes a lot of money from fixing cars that have been in an accident or have slight scratches on them.
To grow his business we made a list of all car dealerships in his city.
We also contacted a business at the port that oversees the import of a lot of used and salvage cars.
We calculated that he could afford to spend thirty dollars on marketing to acquire a new customer.

We printed little coupons with the client's logo on them.
What we did next was to create an offer on a card that said,

"We would like to help your customers by fixing their cars and giving them new paint jobs.
For everyone you refer to us, we will pay you thirty dollars if that individual pays for any of our services.

In addition to this, we will pay you thirty dollars more every single time that individual comes back to us for the next 12 months.
This means, if you refer someone to us and they come to us 6 times in the next 12 months, you will make 180 dollars for just that one referral. Imagine you send us 10 people with that same arrangement, you will receive 1800 dollars for not doing any work. "

This campaign was an absolute success.
The last time I spoke with the owner of that business, he told me he was planning on expanding overseas.

That is an example of using Mutually Beneficial Leverage.
Let me teach you how to use this strategy in your business.

The key is to find someone who already has your customers and to come to an arrangement that is mutually beneficial.
Why struggle to find new customers one by one when someone else has already spent money and time to do that work?

Step 1
Look for a Host
This is a business or individual who your ideal customers buy from or interact with on a consistent basis.
I use the word host in reference to someone or a business that is hosting your ideal customers. As in the host of a party or event.
Imagine all your ideal customers are assembled in one room.
This business or individual should be offering products or services that compliment yours.
For example a Real Estate agent can be a great host for an entrepreneur who owns a carpet cleaning service. And vice versa.
If you are the carpet cleaner, it is likely that many of your ideal customers own homes.
What you do is to go to the Real Estate Agent and present her with a deal that will benefit both of you.

What products do people buy before, with or after they purchase your product?
If you sell heavy duty tractors, maybe your customers buy insurance and fuel somewhere in that cycle.

If you sell shoes, your customers also buy suits, shirts, socks and belts. If you sell fitness programs, your customers buy dietary supplements, exercise equipment and clothing.

If you sell food, your customers buy drinks and desserts as well. If they do not buy them from you they are probably buying from someone else.

Write down the names of 7 businesses and individuals who are hosts to your ideal customers

1
2
3
4
5
6
7

Step 2
Offer the mutually beneficial deal
There are endorsement deals and distribution deals.
Distribution deals are more effective and you can see immediate results. It is the same as having another business work for you.

Endorsement deals
The genius in this strategy is that you have to promise to give the host residual income even after the first transaction.

Secondly you have to let the host know what is in it for them specifically

Saying "You will make money every time you refer someone" is not as good as

"For every 1000 paying customers you send us, we will pay you $7000 for those referrals."

The clearer you paint the benefit, the more likely the host will agree.

Distribution deals
This is where the host sells your product or services as an add-on or bonus with their product.

For example, a chef can sell another vendor's cookware as part of his meals.

A speaker can sell another speaker's books or courses along with his as a bundle.

If you sell an information product, you can look for a host who sells a physical product.
If you sell a physical product, you can look for a host who sells an information product.

Scenario-
Let's say you sell books and you find a host who has a school with 10,000 students a year.
Every time the host gets a new student, the school will sell your book to them for you.
That just gave you 10.000 new sales that you didn't have to go and look for.

The way to compensate the host in this case is to offer a profit share or affiliate agreement.
It may say;
"For every book you sell, my profit is 8 dollars. I will give you 5 dollars for every sale. For 10,000 books, your school will make 50,000 dollars more per semester. "
In this case, you just made $30,000 worth of sales without leaving your home and you just got new customers who now know your name.

Step 3
Try this out with only 3 hosts to start with.
Once you see results, tweak it to fit your style and business model and repeat the process once a month for 12 months.
Remember the steps and scripts I have shared with you.
1 Find a host
2 Offer a mutually beneficial endorsement or distribution deal
3 Repeat with other hosts

Leveraged Appearances

When a guest preacher is invited to speak to a congregation of 50,000 people, he automatically gets access to an audience that may be ten times what he has had in the last 12 months.

This why PR and having an effective content strategy is so effective in our time.

The Internet has provided the greatest content distribution vehicle known to man.

Whenever I accept a speaking engagement, my words are no longer confined to a conference or Church auditorium.

Tweets, Facebook posts and Social media in general can spread my words farther than any other medium I could have paid for.

Take Warren Buffett as an example.

He has positioned himself as the greatest teacher of investing in our time.

Berkshire Hathaway's annual general meetings attract over 40,000 people.

He gets to speak, teach and influence an indoctrinated audience who own shares in his business and many of them buy more after they listen to him.

Warren is a master at this form of leveraged lead generation.

He has had op-eds and speaking engagements at business schools for the last 5 decades.

Another person who understood this well was Steve Jobs.

Imagine if Apple had announced that they wanted journalists to come and hear them talk about products. How many people would have responded?

Apple has conferences and events where they get literally educate millions of people on their new products and then they close with a call to action.

The genius of this is that people travel and spend hours to listen to a two hour sales pitch.

Absolute genius.

I reckon WWDC is one of the most watched webinars every year. The beauty of this is that Apple doesn't say it's a webinar.

I advise entrepreneurs to look for speaking engagements that will get them in front of potential clients.

Unfortunately, many people take any speaking engagement regardless of whether it will be an opportunity for lead generation.

Leveraged Direct Response Advertising

My years of running an Advertising business taught me that you can either turn Advertising into profit or a liability.

Many entrepreneurs want to copy big brands like Coca Cola and Nike because they like the ads they see but mostly because they are ignorant.

They don't realize that there is a difference between brand advertising and direct response advertising.

Brand advertising is when your bank publishes an ad that shows how long they have been in business and how many cities they cover.

Many big brands only do this kind of advertising because they believe people will buy if they are always seeing your brand online or on TV.

Smaller businesses copy this because they don't know that much of that kind of advertising produces no results.

In fact the advertising agencies can't even tell you if their work increased sales and by what percentage.

This is why advertising has such a bad name in many circles.

Direct response advertising on the other hand is when you see an ad that asks you to call or text or email to get an offer.

Your call is a "direct response" to their offer.

The business can then say that, "we spent $9,000 on this medium and it produced $50,000 in sales. If we tweak our offer for higher conversions, we can spend more and earn more."

An important point to note is that you should only advertise in a medium that will provide the highest upside and attract the specific market that you are targeting.

People make the mistake of advertising in general publications when they would have made more money by sticking that same ad in a focused trade publication.

Even celebrities are walking billboards that are many times a waste of money.

I saw the product launch of a fashion brand recently that chose a celebrity who doesn't appeal to their audience.

To make matters worse, the celebrity herself has never been seen publicly wearing the brand since the launch.

There are specific mediums that target groups such as plumbers, millennials, preachers, speakers, politicians, doctors, retailers, baby boomers and even recently married couples.

It's your job to find out what these are and send your offer to them.

Part 2- **Seven Marketing Strategies that work and Picking the right ones for your business.**

1 A Jack of all trades never builds an empire

If I gave you $10 million dollars today and asked you to only focus on one aspect of your business, one customer segment and marketing strategy, what would your answer be?

For many people, these are the only conditions under which they would do what they truly love.

Think of all of the most profitable businesses you know of. Each one is primarily known for one kind of product.

No matter how many other types of products they have, there are a few that take up the majority of their time, energy and resources.

I know of no long term successes who are not focused on one vision.

This is also a great strategy because you can out-innovate your competition when they are trying to do too much.

You can decide on which niche or high value activity will bring you the greatest returns in the long term.

If you can't describe what you do in one sentence, it is likely that you are doing too much.

What is your single vision?

What is your single message?

Who is your ideal customer?

2 Invest In Content That Educates and Shares Wisdom Not Just Information

One time Jesus made a statement that every marketer should memorize. When asks why he spoke to the Jews in parables, he responded:

For the hearts of this people have grown dull.
Their ears are hard of hearing,
and their eyes they have closed,
lest they should see with *their* eyes and hear with *their* ears,
lest they should understand with *their* hearts and turn,
So that I should heal them. Matthew 15:15 NKJV

What he was saying was that the healing the people desired depended on what they saw, heard and understood.

This is content strategy 101.

You can't influence people to buy from you if they don't understand your message.

Many businesses have all kinds of content but don't see a return because they are sharing information and not wisdom.

Information has its place but most people would rather get wisdom.

Information merely informs the audience on the state of affairs. It may motivate or even inspire but it produces little results.

You will find out that a lot of people know what is wrong with the economy or what the government is failing but few know what to do to make it right.

Information says "the system is broken."

Wisdom says "press the red button to fix it."

Your customers don't just want 4 ways to invest in real estate. They want to know how much to invest and what returns to expect.

A professional services business that does not have a newsletter is either irresponsible or doesn't care much about its market.

Education positions your brand as an authority.

The person your prospect calls "Teacher" is the one who will get her money.

A dentist or chiropractor who does not have a consistent stream of content going out to prospects may as well wait for his competition to take over the market.

3 Targeting your offers

Both the Toyota Prius and Tesla range of electric cars are in the same market.

If you look closer you will realize that they serve different kinds of people.

The Tesla is more of a status symbol than the Prius.

It caters to the segment of the market that wants a more technologically advanced and aesthetically appealing vehicle.

The toothpaste being sold in your corner store is targeted at different customer segments as well.

There are tubes that cater to those who want fluoride and those who don't. Other types cater to those who want mint but no baking soda or those who want baking soda but no Peroxide Fluoride.

This book has wisdom that will benefit all kinds of business owners but I decided to focus on high paid advisors, coaches, consultants and the professional services segments. This book focuses on entrepreneurs and business owners.

Why do you think I did that?

I understand those segments better than many others so I decided to focus on them in this book. This way I deliver more value to my market than any other competitors can.

You should take a look at your products and find a way to niche them for your highest value clients.

Many times your highest value clients are those whom you understand deeply.

The client who feels like you understand her will be motivated to buy from you.

4 Pick the highest value products and customers

One of the biggest mistakes I have ever made is picking the wrong client.

I sometimes mistakenly thought the client was the one picking me.

My first client paid me about $700. The next client paid about $2000. The one after that paid about $300.

Later I was able to increase my fee from about $1,500 to $50,000, depending on the project.

One day I sat down and decided to focus on clients for whom I could provide the most value.

I looked at my past clients and identified the ones for whom work was fun and energized.

I also identified the ones who may have paid more but were a drain on my emotions and resources.

What I did next was look at which products and services were producing the bulk of my revenue. To my surprise these were the products that I enjoyed delivering the most.

A focus on what works made all the difference.

The interesting thing is that for the same work, I can produce 10 times the results by focusing on a client who will benefit more.

Your business or practice has a few products and customers that should take up all your focus.

Do the same exercise and you will have less stress and more growth.

5 Launching a new product

Whenever you are about to launch a new product, always think about the client first.

What the client wants should be your first priority.

Secondly, determine what your message is going to be.

Third, write down your offer and the benefits that will attract the prospect.

Fourth, decide on which medium you will use to deliver your offer

Fifth, make sure your funnels, systems and sales sequences are optimized before you send out the offer. This will include contacting partners and affiliates to make sure they send out your offer to their clients in a synchronized fashion.

You can use this formula and you can double your sales in mere months.

6 Setting up sales funnels and sequences

When you buy from Amazon or any efficient business, they put you into a sequence or funnel.

This determines how many emails or offers or phone calls you will receive from them over the next few months.

Some businesses will send you a gift on your birthday and an offer on every major holiday.

I have seen profitable businesses that have over one hundred steps in their funnel.

They know what their clients want and deliver great value on a weekly or monthly basis.

At our workshops, we make sure to build out funnels because this automates your business without having to hire extra staff in many cases.

In some businesses, an efficient sales funnel may even cause you to not need some of your team members.

Here is a simple funnel for a Financial Services Company

Step 1 Send direct mail to prospect (lead magnet)

Step 2 Client responds to offer and calls for consultation. (Opt-in form)

Step 3 Client pays for service (Value delivery)

Step 4 Client receives bonus offer (One click upsell)

Step 5 to Step 9 Client receives value packed email on investment strategies two times a week

Step 10 Client receives offer

Step 11-Step 14 Client receives free trial of new service

Step 15-Step 19 Client receives more free content

Step 20 Client is introduced to affiliate offer

Step 21-40 free high value content twice a week

Etc. etc.

Do you see how this works?

For many people, their fear is that the client will get angry if they receive too much communication.

In my experience, the better qualified your client is, the more willing they will be to hear from you.

We all dislike spam but there are newsletters that we want to receive every week because of how useful the content is.

In fact, the higher priced your services are, the less the client complains unless you abuse their permission.

7 Find comparisons that made your product look good

I have a media and technology business so I am very familiar with hacker schools. Part of the reason I am familiar with them is that I setup a school to teach STEM and Entrepreneurship to African youth.

In my research I found out that many hacker schools, no matter how small have a habit of comparing their acceptance rate to Harvard or some other high priced institution.

Initially I thought no one would fall for it I was wrong.

I spoke with some students who attended hacker schools and many of them bragged about how their school only accepted 0.5 percent of the applications.

The funny thing is that if you receive 500 applications and only admit 30 students, you can't really compare that to the application pool at Harvard.

But like I said, I was wrong and you can do that comparison.

The reason you can do this is because people want to believe something.

But more importantly, they want a justification they can publicly address.

There are programs in many business schools that you can join by simply paying the fee. They don't even have strict laws on whether you have a degree or not.

Many smart business owners have taken these courses and have photos of them in class to prove to their market that they should be taken seriously.

I usually advise clients not to fall for credentials but people tend to like that their lawyer is Ivy league trained and has worked in New York City. Whether he is good at what he does is usually given second place.

Figure out a comparison that is truthful and yet amplifies the value of your product.

Books can be compared to conferences.

Courses can be compared to masterminds.

2 What prize do you want?

In one of my first businesses, my 3 co-founders and I were offered $2,000 and a showroom that could be turned into a retail space.

The investor was a friend's father and he wanted 51 percent of the business.

The not so funny part about this is that one of my co-founders actually considered the deal.

I wasn't involved in that meeting but this is what I would have asked the investor.

If we give you 51 percent of this business, do you have the resources or insight to assure us that our stake will be worth at least 10 times more in the near future?

Today, I frequently get questions from students who have been offered a deal from an investor and they want to know if they should take it or not.

I always tell them to think like an investor.

If you are going to give away 10 percent of your equity, what is the return on investment?

If you are going to spend $80,000 on a consultant, can she guarantee that you will make $800,000 more in the next 18 months? (I charge about that much for my annual clients and I make that promise)

The next time you hop on a flight to attend a conference or meeting, ask yourself what the return on investment will be.

Most people get so hang up on price and cost that they never dare to venture things that will give them a huge reward later.

They are so focused on today that they can't think big enough for tomorrow.

It reminds me of the story of the two farmers who heard there was gold buried deep in their fields. The gold was supposedly worth millions

Farmer 1-I'm going to sell my tractor and use some of my savings to buy equipment.

Farmer 2- I hear the equipment is really expensive. I'll just stick to farming.

Farmer 1 bought the equipment, got the gold, sold it and bought his neighbor's farmland as well.

You have to train your mind to always consider the prize over the price.

It has to be deliberate and consistently intentional.

Never let challenge or what it will cost to get to your goals, stand in your way.

This is so important that I'll share another true story to drive it home.

On her fortieth birthday, Anita goes to her pastor for counsel.

Anita-Pastor I have always wanted to become a nurse but I never had the money to pay for school until now.

Pastor-Praise God that the money has come. What is stopping you now?

Anita-well…hmm… you see, I just turned 40. By the time I'm done with the course I'll be 44 years old. 4 years is a long time.

Pastor smiles and wonders if he should give her a holy slap…but he restrains himself.

Pastor-Anita, if you don't take the course, how old will you be in 4 years?

Anita- 44

Pastor- You can either turn 44 with a Nursing degree or 44 without one. Which would you prefer?

Remember-Prize trumps price

3 The Fundamental Mental Models for Business Growth

Whenever you are about to launch a product, think of these in this order

1 The customers who want this and are willing to pay for it

2 The offer or appeal that will attract them

3 The message I will tell them that will cause them to pay me

The Marketing Mindset Formula

1 Find the customers who are motivated and willing to pay you for your product (Market)

2 Decide on who you will be to them (Positioning)

3 Decide on what product you will give them to satisfy their desires/pains/problems/goals/ambitions (Product)

How do you attract your ideal customers?

You can use a free stuff, trial, sample, discount, bundle, promotion, social proof, free gift upon purchase etc. We'll talk more about this later. Whatever they find, attractive, make sure you use that as a magnet.

You would be surprised how many people don't know what their ideal customer is attracted to.

4 Setup a step by step strategy of how you are going to attract them and get them to buy from you

All of the above leads to cash in the bank.

1 Market-Feeding the hungry customers who want to pay you

If you were starting a restaurant today, which of these would be the most important to you?

Location

Dedicated Staff

Best chef

Hungry customers who are willing to pay for your food

Did you choose the right answer?

Without people who are willing to give you money, you don't have a business.

As important as all the other things are, nothing is more important than your customers. NOTHING.

Your business will more likely die from not being able to identify what customers want than from any other external factor.

Here is the criteria-

Easy to identify-

When I used to sell shoes, we would think of every male who fit our broad target market as ideal.

That was a mistake.

Instead of focusing on the trees, that is the individual customer segments that we could satisfy the most, we focused on the forest.

When you think of your market, you must have a clear picture of one person or one business that you can focus on.

Here is the description of one of my ideal customers for one of my products-

Joseph is a business owner in his mid-thirties. His business has revenue of over $700,000 a year. He markets online and offline and understands the importance and effective of Advertising when done right. He is committed to developing himself so he reads at least one business book every other month and watching YouTube videos and courses to improve his knowledge. On weekends, he spends the time with his two children. On Sundays, they all go out to eat at a restaurant after Church. He desires more control, freedom and flexibility in his life. He would like to be recognized for his genius and wants to make a difference in the world. The words freedom, prosperity and contribution are words he is comfortable with. Joseph is bold and doesn't have time for excuses. He believes second place is the same as last place and is determined to be the best.

Knowing who Joseph is, helps me to target business owners who fit his lifestyle and aspirations. For example, since I know what he does on most weekends, I know if I should be trying to market to him on a Saturday morning at the office or at home. I also know that he likes Tennis and Soccer so advertising at the Super Bowl may not be the wisest decision.

Describe your ideal customer here

………………………………………………………………………

Easy to find:

In certain markets, there isn't much data available.

You can imagine how difficult it will be to get the names and phone numbers of every street vendor in Mumbai.

Or how much work you will have to do to find out which restaurant owners in Kigali prefer ripe plantains over green ones.

The good news is that many times someone else has already done the work for you.

There are complementary businesses or institutions that are already reaching your ideal customer.

Here is a neat trick-Other people's customers

If your product is targeted at taxi drivers in Accra, there are unions and groups that you can use to reach them.

If you want to reach all real estate developers who need used earth moving machines, there is a chance that the person they buy their cement from is someone to contact or partner with.

There are other tools such as Google Keyword Planner that can help you find online customers.

Someone is already selling to your prospects, find them and you will find your ideal customer.

Who is already selling to your customers?

………………………………………………………………………………
…………………….

Easy to reach:

Your ideal customer must be easy to reach so they can find about you.

The Internet and social media makes it easy for you to reach nearly any kind of customer.

In the case where your customers are not online, there are other ways to get to them such as salespeople, direct mail or in places where they congregate like a Church, school, conference or trade show.

Your ideal customer has books, magazines, TV shows, gatherings and events that she is either attending regularly or watching.

Where can you find your ideal customer today? List magazines, shows, cities, towns, events etc.

....
....

Lovers and friends

When I started setting up referral systems for business owners I realized most of them did not like their customers.

Unfortunately many business owners do not consider their customers as friends.

This makes every transaction a battle of who will win or get the upper hand in this deal.

Every transaction should be a combination of love and value.

You need to decide what kinds of customers you would like to have for the next 10 years.

If you aren't comfortable with the thought of hanging out for hours with a client….or having them around your family, maybe you should consider redefining your ideal customer.

....
....

4 Targets and the fish soup story

A popular chef had always liked octopus soup so he decided to create an entire menu with different kinds of fish soup.

The day he launched the menu, less than 5% of the people bought it.

He later found out that there had been news reports of contaminated seafood at the local market so people in the neighborhood were advised to stay away from seafood for 3 weeks while the matter was resolved.

What happened here?

Many entrepreneurs will decide on what product to create before they find out if anyone wants it.

It's like making fish soup and then asking your customers if they want fried or cooked fish.

The lesson here is to know what your customers want to "eat" and then deliver what they want in your own special way.

NB:

In B2B many business owners make the mistake of thinking that they are selling to an entire business.

This makes them consider the brand and bunch of other factors that won't make or break the deal.

The point to note here is that businesses do not give contracts or sign checks. Whether you are dealing with a government or corporation, understand that you are selling to humans.

The authorization you need for that deal will come from the hand of a human being so put your pitch together thinking of what would make it attractive to a man or woman.

Don't allow yourself to be bullied by someone's brand.

That business you are afraid of can disappear in the next 12 months.

Write down the answers to the following-

What does my ideal customer need?

What does my ideal customer want?

What are his or her biggest hopes, desires and dreams?

What does he fear?

Who does he listen to?

Who does she follow?

What obstacles does he face?

What does she need to do today to get the result she desires?

What am I going to give my ideal customer that is different from what everyone else is?

Who is selling to my ideal customer the most?

What are they doing that works that I am not?

What do I want to be known for in the next 10 years?

5 What is your strategy? What tactics will you need to get there?

I once ran the social media campaigns for a lifestyle brand.
One of the things I did to increase leads and prospects was to use social proof.

Every day I would put up two to three photos of people wearing our products.

After a while our prospects visited our pages daily just to see which of their friends was being featured.

The sad thing is that I didn't have a strategy to back this tactic.

I didn't have any system that would turn these followers into buying customers.

What I should have done was to offer a promotion such as bundle or try-before-you-buy deal to get them into our funnel.

Strategy is what to do and why you're doing it.

Tactics are the how to do it.

For example, a footwear brand's strategy is to be the best selling athletic shoe brand in the world by producing high quality running shoes.

Some of their tactics are TV ads, billboards, and celebrity endorsements and pop up shops.

See the difference?

Strategy is the long term goal with well-defined steps.

Your advertising, social media accounts, speaking engagements, sales pitches, trade shows and product launches are all tactics.

You can't grow a business consistently on tactics.

You need a strategy first and then you can decide on what tactics will help you get there.

Here is a template you can use:

My strategy is to
become ....

I will achieve this by
doing/creating/implementing ....
....

The tactics/techniques I will use are

2

3

4

6 Pricing

When I was in the business of selling luxury products I noticed I had a problem with selling shoes above $500.

At the time I didn't own any clothing that cost more than $500 so I kept putting myself in the customer's shoes.

The truth of the matter is that if I had bothered to look down, I would have noticed that my customer could afford $1000 shoes.

The first lesson here is that you may not be your ideal customer so don't make decisions from that mindset.

Here is another analogy to look at this a little differently.

After college I wanted to be an investment banker.

I had a Computer Science degree but the world of Wall Street and Finance fascinated me.

I had just read Snowball; the Warren Buffett biography so all I could see were dollar signs.

I took classes at the Stock Exchange but I later realized I couldn't see myself doing that every day.

What I learned about who makes money and who doesn't surprised me.

The answer is boldness.

I found out that successful investors usually make more money than their peers because of courage.

Many people wrongly assume that it is information.

Information and intelligence many times doesn't even matter much in cases like this.

In business, your boldness will be tested more times than your intelligence ever will.

You can double your business in less than a year if you just increase prices.

What is stopping you from doing that is all excuses and fear you have given yourself.

The minute you realize you can do whatever you want with your business, you will be free to innovate.

Remember never to price according to poverty or emotions, price according to goals.

Determine what amount you desire you make and price accordingly.

Finally, I have also noticed that people who grew up around wealth find it easier to charge what they want.

This is not always the case but sadly I have also noticed that those who grew up without much struggle with pricing.

7 Life is easier with examples

One of the biggest complaints of business owners when they learn a better way of doing things is, *"that will not work in my business/industry."*

That kind of thinking stifles creativity.

I once heard Kenneth E. Hagin say *"those who think they can and those who think they cannot are both right. "*

It reminds of the Roger Bannister story as well.

Before he run the four-minute mile, many people doubted that it was possible for a human being to run that fast.

I read somewhere that within 5 years, so many people had broken that record that runners started setting their sights on bigger goals.

It's the same in your business.

Everyone usually just copies what is familiar.

Until we see better examples we usually stick to what everyone else is doing.

When I speak to doctors with private practices, I notice they all do the same kind of marketing.

If they notice the chiropractor and dentist next door are paying for online ads, they do the same.

This kind of copycat behavior is the reason customers see most businesses as a commodity with no differentiation.

Do you want to have a competitive advantage that will confuse your competitors?

Do the exercises I am teaching and implement the strategies I am showing you.

Don't overthink these proven formulas I am presenting you.

I guarantee that by the time we are done, you will know more than 70 percent of your competitors are doing.

8 Who are you?

One reason for a lack of productivity is when the entrepreneur doesn't know who she is supposed to be in the business.

When you look at the average CEO's to do list, it is filled with things that will not impact the growth of the business in anyway.

The problem is not the to-do list. The problem is the mindset.

Here are some mindsets you should develop to help you build a profitable business.

You are the visionary

The visionary thinks past providing the needs of his customers.

He thinks of how to satisfy his customers desires beyond their expectations.

If his product is a blender, he will make sure it blends better than the others on the market.

Even better than that, the visionary's blender will be beautifully designed and easy to use.

He has moved past the function and is now appealing to the desires of his customer.

He focuses on quick delivery and innovation because no customer ever said "I would like to buy an ugly looking blender that will arrive at my home 5 weeks after I ordered it."

You think about creating value

Every day you think about how you can serve your customers better.

You are in business to help them become who they want to be.

I'm not just talking about adding features.

I'm talking about building a business and products that your customers will love to tell others about.

Answer this question-

What would you do for your customers if they only paid you for the results?

You work on the business not just in it

You know what your numbers are on a weekly basis.

You know what is profitable and what is not.

You know how much you are spending on Marketing and how much you are spending to get new customers.

You know what the changes in the industry are and you are prepared for them in advance.

You know how if the business is growing and who the top performers are in the company.

You know how much money is in the bank and how much cash you have on hand.

You know if the business grew by 10% or by 500% month on month.

You understand what the system is from product to sale to delivery.

You can go away for 3 months and the business will still grow because you have setup effective systems.

You know who your top 3 competitors are and what they are offering, how much they charge and which segment of the market they are targeting.

You develop your team

Your team members look up to you for structure, vision and direction.

You give them responsibility and set goals for them to achieve.

Which of these mindsets do you need to develop in the next 10 days?

9 Focus + Understanding + Quick Action =Fast Growth

Not everyone spends 12 hours at the office should say that they work 12 hour days.

Many business owners spend their time on things that are not work even though they may be in the office.

I know of a business owner who does not know that going to print brochures and cash checks at the bank is not work.

He spends much of his time doing things that someone else should be doing for him.

He claims to work 80 hour weeks but half of that time was not spent doing anything that will bring a return on investment for the business.

Most people believe time changes things.

That is not always true.

Many are content with small developments.

They would rather go through a forest tree by tree.

The masters of enterprise prefer to fly over the forest.

You have to decide to do away with linear thinking.

You have to be focused on getting results instead of focusing on activity alone.

A student failed his exams and his friends could not understand it.

One of them said, "He was always in the library. How could he fail?"

Finally one student responded, "Traffic is not the same as results".

Today you will decide to get results without excuses.

You should demand the same of your team.

My intern story

I had an intern who had never been challenged this way.

When I would tell him to get me information from a client, he would email the client a few times and quit.

I taught him that emailing the client was just activity.

The result and the proof of work was the information I requested.

The next day he went to the client's office and came back with the information.

On the subject of leverage, I will show you how to make this kind of thinking a habit.

Walking with a billionaire

A young businessman approached a billionaire asking him for help.

The billionaire said,

"Young man, I'll make you a deal. I will walk with you across that street in the presence of the people you would like to do business with. When we are done, there isn't a single person who will not accept your business.

As the story goes, when others saw that this young man had the ear and approval of the billionaire, they believed he must be someone important.

This story is an example of leverage.

It is choosing an action that will return the results of a multitude of actions.

It is flying to your destination instead of walking.

It is a force multiplier.

A **force multiplier** *refers to a factor that dramatically increases (hence "multiplies") the effectiveness of an item or group. Some common* **force multipliers** *are: Morale. Technology—Wikipedia*

I will show you how to find force multipliers so that one action can return double or sometimes even ten times the results that you once expected.

This was my Road map To Business Success

1 Identify high value, high paying clients.

2 Only do the most productive activities to help them.

3 Attract more of them with an automated Marketing system.

This is the exact sales sequence that took me from struggling business owner to respected authority

1 Create a lead magnet that demonstrates value.

2 Deploy an offer that takes away risk and promises more value.

3 Close the sale by using mental triggers to convert the prospect.

These Are the 3 Main Traffic Sources I Use

1 Leverage via joint ventures, collaborations and affiliates

2 High Impact Appearances, speaking engagements and workshops

3 Highly Targeted Advertising campaigns

Why I Am Sharing My Secrets

I started my first business in Ghana with zero capital and today I am blessed to be able to charge fees of $50,000.

I know a lot of business owners who are working all the time, losing sleep, precious family time and have little to show for their labor.
I hope my story will do two things.
First, it will not only inspire but give you a step by step road map to finally living the life you dream of.

Secondly, whenever I share my story, I attract clients and students who want me to help them achieve the same results. At the end of this presentation I'll offer you a chance to do the same.

HOW THE BEST DO A FEW THINGS AND GET MAXIMUM RESULTS

Dear Ambitious Founder,

I know it's easy to get overwhelmed and do too much at the same time.

Do you know which activities provide the greatest leverage for your business?

If not, keep reading.

The central purpose of Growingstartup.com is about **to show business owners–**
How to do the few things that bring the greatest results.
That's it.

Instead of getting overwhelmed by the latest gimmick or too much to do…

There are a few high leverage, high profit activities that will accelerate your personal and business growth.
Just like you I also have clients in almost every country on earth: China, Australia, England and right here in the USA.

Business has truly become global for those of us who work in both the offline and online worlds.

If you ever feel overwhelmed with the process getting your business in order…

If you ever feel like you are not getting the right customer or that you are doing too much for too little…

If you feel like your customers aren't responding to your Marketing and Advertising like they should…

You should be getting more respect than you currently have…

Let me show you how to start growing your startup, attract paying customers and multiply your profits.

I'm very fortunate to work with founders as private clients for 6 figure fees–

And 15 percent of the extra revenue that I bring them.

The key to all of this is to deliver more value than the money you receive.

Write that down and never forget it.

My belief is that most business can grow with only these three pillars.

- Pillar 1 Getting prospects to pay attention to you.
- Pillar 2 turning those prospects into buyers.
- Pillar 3 Doing a great job and getting those buyers to become repeat buyers.

Here is how to get started-

1 Know what your perfect customer wants

It's very important for you to know your customer.

What do they want? Where do they want to go?

What will they become after using your product?

How can you help someone you don't understand?

2 Instant results with over-the-top value

We both know that people are naturally skeptical.

Many businesses promise and then they fail to deliver.

There are numerous reports of bad customer experience and client complaints.

This is good for you because you can find out what the biggest questions are in your customer's mind. And answer them in advance.

You overcome their objections by demonstrating how you can help them.

Simple right?

The reason someone comes to you is because they hope to move closer to their ultimate desire.

You should always put your best foot forward by starting a relationship with high value.

When highly respected chefs create a menu, they don't start with mediocre food.

They give their best value from the first course.

Give people what they can use to get the results they seek immediately.

Always start with your best value.

3 Offer proof to dissolve their doubts and build a connection

I'm sure we can both agree that it is easier for us to make buying decisions after we have seen it work for someone else.

Show past experiences to demonstrate that other people just like them got outstanding results.

Testimonials. Endorsements, syndication and social proof are a powerful way to turn prospects into paying customers.

I'll show you how to use syndicated distribution to double your revenue in record time.

4 Give the Tools and Do the Work for Them

Would you rather pay for the food or for the recipe?

Most people would rather pay for the food.

Your customers are the same.

As much as possible, give them what they want with as little steps as possible.

People prefer for products to be intuitive and done for them.

Don't hold back. You will make more by doing this while your competition is struggling to catch up.

What can you give your customer today to get them one step closer to their desired outcome?

5 How to Get a Prospect to Buy

What we have been doing so far is moving your customer closer to their desired outcome.

What you do next is to let the customer know that they will receive accelerated results when they use your product, sign up for your program or subscribe to your service.

You are simply making an offer such as a free trial, sample, bundle, promotion, risk reversal or an amazing guarantee to remove all fears from buying

This is literally like holding their hands as they pull out their wallets to pay you.

Note:

For this to work, you need to genuinely care about your customers and to be delivering value ethically.
This is not a get rich quick scheme.

Personally I believe in long term results.

The great news is that you don't even have to have a large customer base to succeed.

Until now, no one has taught you the consistent way to grow and retain customers who are interested and willing to pay you.

I'll show you quicker ways to get outstanding cash flow and consistent profits.

What you are going to get is an actual campaign that I have used and many others have used to sell a ridiculous amount of goods and services.

You will learn online and offline persuasion, business growth systems and marketing strategies that multiply sales.

I can help you *but —You've got to take the first step*.
Thank you for reading.

INCREASING SALES AND REPEAT CUSTOMERS AT A BARBERSHOP BUSINESS

This past weekend I visited a new barbershop with my brother in law and his son. I usually look out for the fastest barber in the room whenever I go to a new place for a haircut. I do this because I think of time like a currency most times. 30 minutes at the barber's is 30 minutes that can be used to read, work, minister to someone or engage in some other activity that may be more profitable. Time should be invested and not spent since it's the same as spending your life.

Anyway back to the story. This is about how to grow a barbershop business and other life lessons we take for granted.

When it was my turn I proceeded to ask the barber if he could complete my haircut in 10 minutes. I saw my bro in law cringe a little because he didn't want us to offend the guy. The barber (let's call him Kenny) said he didn't want to rush it so I sat down anyway and hoped it would take about 20 minutes. That was terribly presumptuous of me. Lol

In between barbershop banter, charging a client's phone, eating chips (Kenny did not me) and receiving a pretty good haircut, I observed the other barbers in the room and noticed they were simply giving haircuts and letting the clients leave without taking any details to follow up later with other value added services. After my haircut, Kenny thanked us, took our money and that was it. Since I teach people how to start and grow businesses I'll share what I think Kenny and his other mates could have done to increase their revenue.

1. Customer data

my bro in law has been to that barbershop many times with his son but no one knows their details. Kenny should have taken down our numbers or email addresses. With these details I would call, text or email the a link to my professional Twitter page or blog where he shares insights on personal grooming, style or creating a personal brand as a young black man.

I say this because Kenny is not just in the haircut business. He is in the personal grooming, style and image management business. The more he acts as an expert in these areas, the more credibility he will have.

2. Value Creation and Marketing

I would call or email or text the client every two weeks with facial and skincare tips as well as a reminder to come by the barbershop since I'm sure they may need a shave or haircut soon. I would recommend (and sell) products such as shaving gels and other skincare products to the client. Since I'm this case my brother in law visits this barbershop with his son, I would create Father/Mother and Son packages that cater to parents who bring their sons to the shop. I would also collaborate with service providers whose services would appeal to young boys. I may even go as far as selling Star Wars, Pokémon or whatever merchandise these parents usually buy for their sons.

Conclusion

having the skills to cut hair, build a bridge, write code or whatever gift you are trained in is not enough. In a barbershop, what determines success in the long run is not the skill alone but the value the barber provides. The barber who talks to you and advises you on what to do to have healthy hair or skin is ten times more valuable than the one who just cuts your hair. The barber whose goal is to have the happiest customers will find out which of them prefer longer or shorter times in his chair and will tailor his services accordingly.

Value is only value when it benefits the receiver.

By the way, Kenny spent about 50 minutes on my hair that day.

THE METHOD I USE TO READ A 300 PAGE BOOK IN 2 HOURS WITHOUT SPEED READING.

Yes. I can teach you how to read a 300 page book in only 2 hours without speed reading.
Yes. You can do this with eBooks as well.

An old buddy reminded me to share my insights on how to read a 300 page book in 2 hours or less using strategic reading methods. I was taught these principles a few years ago and it has greatly improved many parts of my business. Thanks to a gentleman called Tommy Offe. I have also personally shared these methods with people of varying ages and even languages on 3 continents. Thanks to John Mark

Gladstone Jr for reminding me to share these. I also recorded a voice note for him that I will share here. Click this link for the voice note.

Below is the simple template that I and many others use. It is based largely on Inspectional reading.
I will go into more depth on this in a later post but you can check out Mortimer Adler's How to Read a Book: The Classic Guide to Intelligent Reading (A Touchstone book)
It will give you a primer on some reading methods.

Strategic and Value Driven Reading Template
Name of Book/Article/Blog:
Author:
Date:

1. **Purpose/Goal**

Why are you reading this book/blog/article? What can you use this information for? (Please list your reasons)
E.g. I am reading this book gain insights on sales and marketing ideas I can use for my business.

-
-
-
-
-

2. **Quantitative goal**

E.g. am going to retrieve 80% of this book in 2 hours.
-

Preview

Please tick off each section below as you complete them

2. Copyright Date

3. Number of Pages

4. Look at the Cover and Back of the book

5. Conclusion and Introductory paragraphs

6. Content page/Table of Contents

7. Headings, Sub Headings, Pictures, Tables, Equations, Charts

8. Trigger Words/Index -Look through the index and curate 20 to 30 of the most frequent and important words throughout this document.

9. Summary-What is the writer's main argument? In your own words, why did the author write this book?

_____

_____

....
....

10. 10 Points of interest

Read the 10 interests that fit your purpose based on Number 6 in the Preview. (These pages have to be of interest to you)

-
-
-
-
-
-

Extra: To Do

What can I do with this information? How can I apply this information to my life? What are the principles? What are the examples that I can improve upon?

I always write down my To-Do because you are only wise if you use the knowledge you have acquired. Just having a lot of information is not very useful.

I will explain in later posts, other details that will help you read at least 5 times faster than you currently do and still comprehend what you just read.

HOW TO CHOOSE FRIENDS AND BUSINESS PARTNERS

My dad once said "If you are the smartest person amongst your friends, you are not very smart". What he meant by this was that a smart person keep friends who are smarter than him. He went on to tell me a story about how he started his first business in his teens. He had been working with his father for a while but felt it was time to go out on his own.

On one of my grandfather's weekend trips, he moved out because he was too scared to do it while Grandpa was in town. By that time my father had figured out what business he wanted to start and had done all the research he needed. He later spoke to his father who unwillingly agreed. In about 3 years, my father had a profitable business, two cars and was very content as a 22 year old. His only problem was that he felt he was not advancing fast enough. He was doing better than most of his friends and he felt there was more.

One of his buddies had been recommending that he move to a new neighborhood so he finally acquiesced and relocated. My father tells me that the decision to relocate changed his life. He said his new neighborhood was full of young, upwardly mobile professionals who were ambitious to boot. One thing led to another and before he knew it, he was invited to the local Full Gospel Men's Fellowship. He said he had never seen so many zealous and successful believers in his life. They had more than he did and yet they were more engaged in the spiritual things in life. He was challenged to give and contribute more to the world through that season of his life. He still credits much of his early success to having friends who were more developed spiritually, mentally, socially and financially than he was. The smarter his buddies were, the better the conversations he got to engage in and the more challenged he was to live a value driven life.

Many of us keep friends based on familiarity and experience. Why is she your friend? *"I have known her since we were little."*, *"He really listens to me when I talk and he also loves video games."* These answers are good but incomplete. A better reason to keep a friend is to keep people who are going in the same direction as you are at least spiritually and mentally. The person's proximity to your home and business are or minor relevance. For example, a childhood friend who laughs at your dreams without offering good alternate suggestions can be an acquaintance but not a friend.

A friend should be someone concerned with your progress in life. You want the kind of person who is moving forward and does not want you to be left behind. You want the kind of person who will recommend books, seminars, sermons and courses. The friend who will correct any anomalies in your value system is the best kind of friend. When a person bribery, favoritism or any behavior that is not consistent with the Bible, you should reconsider your criteria for friendship.

Acquaintances are many but friends are usually few.

How to Pick Friends and Partners That Will Prosper You

1. Find out what the person's vision is. A person who does not know where they are going will either move slowly in life or go quickly in the wrong direction. I usually prefer having people who think bigger than I do. If you already have a friend or business partner who is not sure of their vision, do your best to help them get on the right road and to start thinking right? David Oyedepo's book on Success Systems is an excellent read. You can get your copy Success Systems here.

2. Pick people who are going in the same direction as you are

if you are planning to start your own business, find friends who have the same dreams or have already started theirs. A friend whose ambition is to climb the corporate ladder may be useful in other scenarios but not when you need to make some critical decisions. Before I started my own business, I worked as an intern. I quickly realized not everyone would be able to help me on my journey. I would hear stuff like "if we all start businesses, who will be an employee". The only people who said this to me were those who had never started a business. There is nothing wrong with being an employee unless it is not your God-given assignment. For me, it wasn't so I found people who had taken the path I was planning on pursuing.

2. Pick people who are not easily impressed

    When I was a teenager, I had a friend (let's call him Joseph) who never found anything impressive. Many of our other friends said this was a sign of arrogance since Joseph was not impressed by the money, cars and clothes most of our peers were drooling over. I never understood this until we got to college. I found out Joseph's father was a millionaire. In his home, the conversations were usually about things that were higher than the average teenager's ambitions.

    Today, I constantly look out for people who are not easily impressed so I can listen to them. This is a good heuristic for picking employees and business partners. If your business partner wants to make his first million dollars and retire at 35, he may not be the right fit for a person who wants to provide value for billions of people and receive billions of dollars a year. At some point, your goals are bound to clash. In addition to this, stay away from partners who over celebrate little achievements.

    A colleague once had a partner who would do anything for a celebrity. He would go as far as giving away free products to anyone who the media recognized as a celebrity regardless of the implications to the business' bottom line.

3. Pick people who act the same regardless of their audience

if you all your closest friends/partners were in the same room, would you have to pretend to support certain views or opinions? If you are against something but have to pretend you are not when before certain people then your moral character is weak. That is really another way to say you are a hypocrite. No one should assume you believe something you do not just because you want to please someone.

4. Pick people with high moral standards

I was considering a collaboration with an old acquaintance from high school. I was planning on going over to his office but decided to speak with him over the phone first. He told me how his business had been prospering recently and a few minutes into the conversation, he said "you know in this country, you have to pick a political side and take care of the right people financially.

That is what we have been doing." It's safe to say I knew we could never work together because I do not believe anyone can build a globally relevant business by doing business based on political connections and palm greasing (bribery). He called it gratuity but it was really corruption.

5. Most Importantly Pick A Person Who Has A High Reverence For God And Loves Jesus.

I am not saying you should only pick religious people to do business with. I don't think it's wise since a believer is supposed to be a light to the world. We are to influence the world with the love and power in us. Separation is when you are in the midst of worldly people but do not act or think in the same manner as they do. A person who respects God and loves Jesus will be more concerned about pleasing God than men. This combination of values will guide this person to usually do things with the best intentions in mind.

Once I tried to partner with someone who had a habit of insulting preachers online. I tried to overlook that since I needed a technical partner. A few days before we could sign an agreement, I asked him about what his thoughts were on money and I quickly realized I was setting myself up to partner with someone who would not make the best financial decisions based on his belief system. In my experience I find a person's belief system permeates everything they do.

Conclusion

My thoughts on how to choose friends and financial partners in this post deals only with the soft issues. In the case of partners, technical competence is very important.

Just because someone is your rich cousin, does not make them a good business partner. Interestingly, good friends produce more good friends since like-minded people usually flock together. Do you have any insights or experiences to avoid when picking friends and partners?

HOW TO USE DIRECTION AND CERTAINTY TO CONVERT PROSPECTS INTO BUYERS

Have you ever seen any advertisement or promotion that offers promises like these "3 easy steps to a better golf swing"—?

"7 ways to become a better manager"—

"3 simple negotiation techniques for salespeople"?

Mobile Application developers have found out that by reducing the number of times someone has to tap their screens to get a certain result, the higher the engagement and user retention. The reason these are so successful is because people will pay for certainty.

The more uncertain someone is about what your product will do for them, the less inclined they will be to buy.

As humans we have a fascination with maps, blueprints, formulas, tips and advice.

We will do almost anything to clear up doubt from our minds. When someone tells you something you don't believe, you either go online to find the answer or ask someone else's opinion.

Successful companies know that their websites, retail space and sales materials should offer step by step instructions.

The mind will always seek the clearer option because it doesn't want to be in darkness.

Offer step by step instructions to your prospects.

People should know what to do if they want to buy something, speak to someone, try your product or have it delivered.

The simpler it is to find the BUY button, the more sales you will make. Give them formulas, tips and steps to success.

No one ever bought anything and said "I bought this because it was so difficult to use".
Everyone brags about things that are easy to use.
What are some other ways you can use certainty in your Marketing to grow your business?

USING MENTAL HACKS TO SELL WITHOUT TRYING TO CONVINCE CUSTOMERS

There are annual competitions that test memory.

One of the former memory champions is an accountant who could look at 52 cards in 24 seconds and tell you exactly what he saw and in the order in which he saw them. He uses a mental hack system.

One famous memory expert was recorded on television as he was introduced to about 200 people in the audience.

He then went ahead and recited their names verbatim from memory.

Wouldn't you like to be able to do that?

I'll show you how… and then I'll share how you can use this to sell products…

Chances are you already know this method but have not made a conscious system out of it.

What many memory experts do…?
They look at an object or event and then they mentally associate it with a story, number or image.

For example, the next time you meet someone called Dannie for the first time, you can associate her name with the word "dancing" or a fruit or a flower that is familiar to you.

Think of your mind as a big room with a lot of mental hooks or coat hangers. You can hang whatever you want for latter recollection.

Now the marketing part….
I heard a successful strategist say "People don't buy because they understand you. People buy because they feel understood."

Let's define that….

The people I speak with most often are those with whom I share similar traits or interests.

I can guess that this is true for you as well.

Whenever we meet a stranger with similar views on important topics or tastes in music, food or TV shows, our minds immediately cast a favorable light on the person.

If this is true then there must be a way to use this human trait to turn your ideas into profits.

Interests are really just mental hooks

If shared interests or a sense of relation can trump years of familiarity, then we can use it to attract people and convert them into buyers.

I learnt this from Jesus Christ and Apostle Paul.
When they spoke with fishermen, they had what I call Hooks of relation.
They would say things that their audience could relate with.
When they spoke with fishermen, they would give analogies such as fishes and nets.
When speaking with people who understood agriculture, they would bring up sheep and pasture.

When someone says "I don't get what you're saying", it means they have searched through their mind and didn't find any image, word or familiar hook to associate your conversation with.
Politicians are exceptionally good at figuring out what mental hooks register with their audience and then repeating those words in order to get a vote.

For example, when speaking with the middle class, you talk about hope and how their dreams will become reality. They will be able to get better jobs, afford new homes, have more significance and pay less taxes.
When speaking with people who are already wealthy, you talk about how their wealth will increase… how you will create systems to help them expand their enterprises and how you will do everything to protect them from harm which may be in the form of competition or foreigners trying to encroach on their incumbent status etc.

Now do you see the pattern?
When you want to convert someone into buying from you or sharing your view, the underlying principle is the same.
Always start by finding out what they already believe and what mental hooks or pictures they are seeing in their mind.
Once they feel that you see the same things as they do, it is easier for them to believe and pay you.

Conclusion
If your mind already works a certain way, there is a likelihood that you already have a framework that others use unintentionally.

Make a system out of your mental hacks or heuristics and you will increase your conversions.

GIVING RESULTS BEFORE MAKING THE SALE

Car dealerships offer test drives because they have found out that after driving a new car, **the mind gets a taste of what we call Instant Gratification.**
The prospect gets to enjoy what it's like to drive a brand new car without paying for it. This rush of instant gratification plants a seed that is difficult for many people to uproot. After that test drive, people say their current vehicle starts to look and feel old. In many cases they return to trade in their old car or buy a new one.

The quicker you can get someone to experience your product, the easier it will be to persuade them to buy.
I heard of a piano salesman who would come and give his prospects a piano to keep in the home for about a week. By the time he returned to collect it, most of the homes decided to keep the piano and pay for it.

This happened because they had already gotten a taste of what it felt like to have a piano in the home. Their children were already enjoying the piano and were even considering getting lessons. **All this instant gratification made it easy for the salesman to close the sale.**
If his customers hadn't gotten to experience it beforehand, it would have been a tougher sell.

 Free samples, free trials, free consultations, demonstrations and other try-before-you-buy tactics work very well.

What can you give people that will get them to experience the benefits of your product immediately?

HOW TO DO REAL LIFE PRODUCT PLACEMENT ON TV, SOCIAL MEDIA AND MUSIC

Very few of people outside the United States have seen even a quarter of the ads in the States. This makes it even more impressive that you can find so many brand evangelists and fans outside the States.

Do not underestimate the power of marketing through movies, TV shows, YouTube videos and other media that can be shared with the click of a mouse.

Product placement is very effective because it shows potential customers how to fit your products into their daily lives. Show users how they can share your products with family, match it with their sneakers, and display it in their living rooms and so on. Proper product placement in the lives of popular people can also make your brand more visible. Many brands have seen great success by giving the coolest kids on campus free products.

Note that it is not enough to give your product to a celebrity or famous person unless a lot of your target will get to see it. A lot of brands give out free samples to celebrities who have little or no web or press presence. Consider using celebrities or brand evangelists as walking billboards.

We have seen brand ambassadors with no social media account and yet the target is a group who do not read newspapers or magazines. If your target is spending four hours on YouTube, everyday then a magazine ad may not be the best

KELLOGG Marketing Case Study

Another brilliant idea that employs the product placement in real life idea was executed in Sweden by Kellogg. A store offered a free box of Special K to customers who would take a photo and tag it with #nyaspecialk (Swedish for 'new Special K'. All the customer had to do was show the cashier the pic and they would get a free box. The marketing director at Kellogg, mentioned that the Instagram app is more popular in Sweden than Twitter so it only made sense to use Instagram.

The brilliance in this campaign is that Kellogg got access to show the customer's friends what brand of cereal they preferred. Kellogg could have done this with a million dollar advertising budget as well but they realized it was a cheaper and more remarkable way to generate brand awareness.

I would like to mention that campaigns like these may not yield immediate results but with consistency, the payout can be huge. Take car companies for example. They know if they advertise consistently enough, a ten year old who has seen the ads all his life will consider buying car brand X when he or she is 30.

Another thing to remember about advertising is that, it should be measurable now or later.

For TV, it may look attractive for most brands but many do not know how to measure the results they get from TV ads. Many more do not know if they got any results from their television campaigns. The lesson here is not to just buy ad space because you can brag to your friends and competitors that you are in this month's issue of Forbes. Bragging rights should be birthed from results.

If you have a friend who is a musician, try to get him to put your brand name in one of his songs.

People will pay more for established brands because they presume the company's brand name has more to lose if it screws up than they do. Hardly anyone compares the specifications of five different television sets when they can just pick from the top three market leaders. When you are hungry, you will buy from certain restaurants not because they are the best but because they are the most unlikely to be bad.

YOU WANT TO START A BUSINESS, HERE IS WHAT YOU SHOULD DO FIRST.

Let me tell you a story about two businesses I started that failed and how I would do things differently. As you read, you will see which pitfalls to avoid in starting your own business as a creative entrepreneur with passive income.

In my first business, we created one of Africa's first IPhone/IOS apps. We had the idea and in a few months we had launched the app. The praise and reviews came in but we made no money from it. Not even $1 dollar. One of the reasons was that it was 2009 and we did not know how to monetize an app. We could have charged for the app or allowed in-game purchases but no one on the team understood sales or marketing very well.

In fact, I was just excited to have worked on something cool at the time. There's a bigger reason why we did not make any money on the app but let me tell you about another business I started that made zero dollars as well.

Fresh Words Inspired was a blog I started to talk about business about 3 years ago. I like lions so nearly all the posts had an image of a lion. Very soon people were sending me photos of lions. I have always liked the t-shirt industry because it allows your illustrations and designs to receive tangible life on a piece of fabric. There's something really fulfilling about seeing someone wear something you created.

I wanted to monetize the blog and the only way I knew how was to have a friend design a tee and put it up so I did exactly that and guess what? No one bought a single shirt. Not even one. I did not understand how to promote products online so I did what I saw others doing and got no good results. Here is the point I was getting at.

"Not understanding how business or anything for that matter works is the same as walking around in a dark room trying to find something you need." In both of the illustrations I just gave, I was ignorant. I had not studied what it took to promote and monetize software or t-shirts. I was trying to use common sense like everyone else.

> "Common sense will get you common results but understanding will make you see farther than anyone else."

What I should have done was to first *understand the market*, identify who my ideal client was and then create a strategy to monetize the products. I could have also researched to find out who else was making money in their field and sought to understand their business model. For example with the t-shirt company, I never bothered to find out if there were any prospective clients who wanted to buy a tee with a lion wearing a snapback. I just assumed others would like it because I liked it.

Understanding can make you so much money in business. It's the difference between a broke real estate developer and a wealthy one. Many people build apartments, not because they know of a specific demand for the property but because they have a few acres of land and think that is the best way to develop it. A wise developer will first find out if the prospective clients seek condos, apartments, town houses or a hotel. She will first identify what the exact opportunity is before laying one brick. Instead of building and then trying to convince someone to buy, she will find out what they want and build with those specifications in mind. This way, her property will stay at full occupancy while her competition are busy wondering why the market is not responding.

Now that you have decided to start a business or monetize your current online assets such as your blog or website, I am going to give you a step by step system you can follow. If you have any questions, subscribe and send me an email with the subject "Question"

Step 1. Identify your value

God has placed in all of us, the ability to create wealth. We all have something of value that we can **develop**. Everyone I have ever read of or met that has had consistent success over decades is doing what they love. By this I mean they are harnessing gifts that God gave them. They discovered these interests and developed them through reading, practice, internships or apprenticeships.

As a creative person, I was good at a lot of things. Fortunately for me I could understood both technical and non-technical subjects but I did not begin to flourish until I tried my hands at them or read enough about my inklings to know if it was something to consider of not. For example, a few years ago I wanted to be an investment banker so I read [The Snowball: Warren Buffett and the Business of Life](#) and took a 3 month course at the Securities Exchange.

By the end of the course I knew I was not ready for that life so I moved on and tested another interest. The most successful people create businesses out of what they can do in their sleep.
This step is to find out what unique value you should package as a product. To have fulfillment and success in your business, you have to create a product or get into a niche that is authentic to your strengths. God has put in all of us something that this world needs, this is one way to find out what that is.
Write down 3 things you are good at and what skills you already have. e.g.–graphic design, event planning, helping others get interviews, writing resumes, interviewing, designing jewelry, cooking, writing poems, teaching music, making beats, encouraging people etc.
Write down 3 things you know better than most people (this may be something that is so obvious to you but others do not see.)
E.g. blogging, photography, chemistry, passing standardized tests, the inner workings of the legal system, how to fill taxes, how to read 50 books a year etc.
Write down 3 ways your friends describe or introduce you to others. e.g. she dresses really well, she knows how to manage a project better than anyone I know, he can bench press 250 pounds, he is a designer, pastor, he makes cool beats, she speaks so softly you want to tell her everything about your life, he loves movies etc.
Write down 3 things you have been successful at that most people struggle with or would like to achieve. (These are sometimes things that

come very easily to you that you can do it in your sleep.)

e.g. Passing the SAT, starting a business, creating a logo, running 1 mile in 10 seconds, taking free kicks, building a website, painting on canvas, illustration, getting a job at a bank, saving money, filling out lengthy forms, losing weight without going to the gym etc.

Write down 3 skills you already have

e.g. graphic design, copywriting, singing, branding, selling t-shirts,

Write down 3 things you like reading, watching or studying.

E.g. leadership, cooking, sales, Faith and Grace in the Bible, Basketball, Counseling, interior decor and furnishing, strategy, lead generation, speed reading etc.

What can you teach easily?

e.g. fencing, rowing, football, writing love letters, picking out investments, styling outfits, teaching young girls how to use make up

Finally, imagine you have $300million in the bank. In order for you to keep this money, you have to pick a career that you will love. It has to be something you can see yourself doing every day with ease even if no one was paying you for it?

e.g. I'd help entrepreneurs learn how to start and grow businesses online, I'd help nursing mothers know what kinds of workouts to do in order to lose weight, I'd help university graduates find jobs, I'd help CEO's organize their schedules, I'd help retail stores organize their shelves better to convert more customers, I'd help big companies to file their taxes, I would like to help good politicians to plot and execute a successful campaign so the bad ones do not win, I'd like to paint caricatures of famous people, I'd like to help small businesses automate their finances, I'd like to help creative entrepreneurs make money online, I'd like to knit Christmas sweaters etc.

Once you discover what your unique value is, you will understand what problem you are naturally equipped to solve. One of the saddest things in life is to see an individual who is not fulfilling their destiny by working on the wrong thing. I am convinced the reason so many people say their jobs are hard is because they are working on the wrong things. The minute you find out who you are and what you have in you, success will start knocking at your door.

Step 2:

Identify your ideal client: find out who you want to serve, what niche you will fit into best and what unique problems they have.

Do you know what is better than having 1000 new customers? It is having 1000 starving customers. As an entrepreneur you do not want everyone to walk into your office or visit your website. You only want those who are hungry for your product because those people will appreciate your value and will most likely buy from you again and again in the future. Most importantly, starving customers rarely argue over price and will most likely refer you to other people who are as hungry as they are.

I am not a fan of pepperoni pizza even though it may be one of the most popular kinds of pizza. I think most of the ones I have tasted are too salty. For this reason every time I see a pizza place with a buy 1 get one free pepperoni pizza deal I look away. I am not their ideal client. I may even be craving for pizza but at that moment, I am not their ideal client. One of the biggest mistakes I made and I see others make all the time is to first get the idea, create the product and then start looking for clients.

The right way is to find out who wants the product and then tailor your idea to fit paying clients. For example, if the head of the United Nations gave you a contract to supply a nation with drugs for malnourished children, would you go and order 2 ships worth of drugs first or would you first find out which specific vitamins and minerals you need to make sure are in the drugs you are yet to import? *You can call this feeding the hungry, or giving water to the thirsty or clothing the naked. The principle is the same.*
"This is like choosing your destination before you get on a plane."

Many people get this wrong so they start a business or website, create posts, upload content to social media and then wait for money to come. After a while when there's no money coming they post more content or create more products on more social networks. This doesn't work either so they get frustrated and quit or move on to something else that they will inevitably fail at.

The first thing is to do here is to write down (not just in your mind) the specific kind of person or niche or customer segment you would like to cater to. If you were a fish, what specific pond would suit you? Are you a don at helping working mothers get back into the workplace? Are you excellent at helping immigrant professional get 6 figure jobs in healthcare consulting? Or can you literally get any college graduate a resume and cover letter that will help them get an interview with Goldman Sachs?

The better you know what you can do and who needs you the most, the more money you will make.

We are intentionally foregoing building a website and other stuff in week 1 until we get the basics well defined. Even if you have done this before, please answer the questions below and email me within the next 7 days with your answers. Those who answer these questions thoroughly will have a better chance of success.

Who is your perfect audience? Who would you love to serve?

Answer the following-

Who are the hungry?

Who are those you are equipped to serve?

Who are those who can relate with your message you can relate to and who need to hear your message to live a better life or to not make certain mistakes?

Please describe in detail

1. Who he/she is…………………………………………..

2. What does he/she like?

…………………………………………………………..

3. What products and services does he/she buy and use?

4. What does he/she look like?

5. What Instagram pages, websites and blogs does he/she read often?

6. Who does he/she listen to?

7. Where does he/she work?

8. If you wanted to find 10000 people exactly like him/her, where could we do that? Both online and offline examples……………………………..

9. What are some questions she has that you can answer? What problems does she have that you have overcome or can give solutions to because of what you have experienced or read?

Let me show you an example of how I used the above exercise for our Business Growth for Creative Entrepreneurs course. You can answer the questions below as well.

Who is the ideal client? Creative Entrepreneur

What is his/her occupation? Small business owner, fashion designer, chef, developer, freelancer, consultant, stylist, blogger, artist, musician, graphic designer etc.

What is his/her biggest desire and end result? She wants freedom. The ability to quit her job and make enough money doing what she loves…she wants to be able to grow a business that allows her to live the lifestyle she dreams of and not be tied to a desk all day… She wants a step by step system to follow. She wants fame, fortune and recognition for her work

What is his/her biggest problem? He does not know where to start because there are too many books, YouTube videos and courses out there. He's not sure which of them will help her achieve her goals.

How can I help him/her today? By offering a step by step system that takes him from the idea stage through to the marketing, sales and profit stage... I can create a free eBook today that does that and also a detailed course that he can follow every week.

Chris Dixon has a really interesting article titled Founder/Market fit. Many people focus on product/market fit when that should be secondary. Entrepreneurs pride themselves on how many ideas they have but many people are not equipped internally to execute on certain opportunities. Many people get to where the puck is going only to realize they don't have the skills of a professional athlete.

Now you know what you have that this commercially valuable, you need to find out what needs what you are making. Talk to people you have already sold to and find out why they bought from you. Segment them into groups so that you can decide of which group is worth your effort and will pay you what you want. For example when I started out as a brand consultant, I found out that corporate clients who had a sales but no experienced marketing team were willing to pay whatever I asked. There were others who also paid me what I wanted but the marketing manager would waste my time with unnecessary emails and phone calls many times because he wanted to take me on some ego trip to prove he knew his job.

If you are yet to start your business, then one way to find if people will buy what you are selling is to ask them to. Go up to someone you believe is an ideal client and say "I am selling this product/service for $100, you can buy it now." The reason I say you should ask for the money is because many people especially your friends or family out of politeness will say that your idea is great and that they would buy it. Until someone pre-orders your product or gives you money for it, do not take their word for it. I know someone who ordered over $3000 worth of samples because his friends had expressed interest. After the products arrived, those who had showered praise on him were nowhere to be found. All of a sudden they had other financial obligations. This would not have happened if he had done what I am about to share next week.

HOW TO MAKE BETTER BUSINESS DECISIONS

I could have titled this *"How to make sure your market does not determine your profits"* or *"Automated systems thinking for entrepreneurs."*
It would surprise you to know how uncommon it is for most entrepreneurs to prioritize thinking. This is why an **automated mental framework is necessary.**
I agree with Buffett when he says *"I insist on a lot of time being spent, almost every day, to just sit and think. That is very uncommon in American business. I read and think. So I do more reading and thinking, and make less impulse decisions than most people in business. I do it because I like this kind of life."*
Here is what I mean.

When I was starting out, no one told me to focus on results. In fact I did not even know what conversion rates were. I was just in it for the activity. I measured my success by how much money had come in not by how much closer I was to my goal.

How would you know if you are winning if you don't know where you are going?
The problem is that many of us measure our satisfaction by our needs and not on our potential.
Speaking in purely monetary terms I could be making $100 million a year but if my potential is $1 billion then I have failed.

Many times we judge ourselves based on what our industry average is or what success others in our field have had.
This is erroneous thinking and a symptom of the herd mentality.

I like something David Oyedepo said. *"The only place you are permitted to have mates is in school."*
What he meant by this is that the people you call contemporaries will define your limit. You won't rise higher than the "market" you think you are in.

What's the solution?
Having an independent mental framework that is focused on your potential.

Be careful that you do not focus on the demand or size of the market either.

I know people who make less than they should because they believe that's a good amount considering their market size. That again is small thinking.

I heard of a businessman who has less than 18,000 people in his town and yet rakes in millions of dollars a year. He refused to let his market determine his potential.

One of my favorite examples of a potential focused mindset is John D. Rockefeller. While his competitors thought they could trump him by competing in the oil industry, John D. had other plans.

John D. knew his potential was bigger than the oil industry. He said his goal was to "light the world". This helped him innovate magnitudes above those who thought they were his competition. They thought they were running the same race. They did not know he was flying above their heads.

Over the years I have learnt that **it is important to build your own mental framework for decision making in business**.
This framework has to be results based and void of emotion. It must be rooted in first principles and factor in human nature.

You have to know where you are going and what needs to happen in order to get there.

Every serious business person I have read about or met is interested in results.

They know these 3 metrics at the back of their minds.
1. How much revenue is expected this month
2. How much revenue do we have now
3. What is the difference and what needs to happen in order for us to be achieve the results we want.

Notice I didn't say "what you need to do to achieve the results you want."
Entrepreneurs love "doing" stuff because they think of activity first before results.

In step 3 maybe someone else needs to do something and not you. Maybe a certain mindset change must happen and not necessarily a physical action.

For example my business changed overnight when I found out that my mental image of myself was not as highly defined as it should have been.

After I defined who I wanted to be internally, all my actions fell into place.

The secret was not in me doing anything new. It was me "being" internally who I am supposed to be.
The minute you see yourself today as you desire to be, you will know what to do, where to go, what kind of business fits your unique skills and even what books you should not read.

I got this Business strategy from the Bible.
When God wanted to give Abraham children He didn't ask him to do anything. He told him to change his inner image of himself by

changing his name. Abram now had to call himself Abraham, which means father of many nations. He started to see himself with many children and started asking people to address him that way.

Very soon Abraham's body obeyed the words he had been speaking.

Two Fundamental Pillars of Your Mental Framework
I believe you need two fundamental pillars to build this mental framework. First you need to understand human behavior.

Secondly, you need to understand which metrics are important. That you got 1000 sales last week does not mean that was a success. Maybe with better innovation and marketing you should have made 10,000 sales instead.

I like something Warren Buffett said.

"To invest successfully over a lifetime does not require a stratospheric IQ, unusual business insights, or inside information," Buffett said. "What's needed is a sound intellectual framework for making decisions and the ability to keep emotions from corroding that framework. This book precisely and clearly prescribes the proper framework. You must provide the emotional discipline."

Warren echoes what I believe so many people miss because they are listening to the wrong information. I pity entrepreneurs who base most of their decisions on what they read in the media. They assume the reporters are business people like them. Sadly many people who write on business don't know what it takes to start or grow a business. Their job is to report and not to advice. The problem is many reporters will add their opinion to a piece when all they should have done is report the facts.

The market then takes the opinions and acts based on that.

Warren Buffett and Charlie Munger's success from what I can infer has little to do with their knowledge on finance. They like many other successful people before them have learnt that human behavior many times is predictable.

If you know what patterns to look out for, you can engineer your own results.

How does this apply to your business?

1. **Define internally what a life full of victory and success would look like.**

    Does that mental image of yourself have a trillion dollar business? Does she have 4 clients or 4,000? Does he drive an Audi R8 or a Mercedes truck? Does she work on the weekends or not? Is he speaking before crowds of 10,000 or 6,000? What does her average working day look like? Who does she eat breakfast with and where does she have lunch? What kind of house does she live in?

    What you do next is write down what keywords describe your perfect image of yourself. If you are in the internet marketing/media space like I am, you can use these keywords but don't limit them to your industry.

Keywords/Key phrases: 90% conversion rate of highly targeted traffic, billions in yearly profits, information marketing, content strategy, business growth, faith in business, rest, Jesus Christ, Frank Kern, Neil Patel, Mark Zuckerberg, Buffett, Gates, Bloomberg, Oyedepo, SEO, Guest Posts, Give too much value, Innovate with value not with low prices, Automate marketing and sales funnel, Give, give, give and then ask for a sale etc. etc.

Knowing what keywords matter to your journey will help you weed out information that is unnecessary.

2. **Decide which metrics matter to you**

It is said that when most people were focusing on how many signups they had, Mark Zuckerberg told his team they would focus on active users. This is a focus on results. If you visit the gym twice a day and yet have the results of someone who goes in only once a month, your activity doesn't mean much.

As an entrepreneur customer satisfaction and conversion rates are excellent metrics to focus on.

3. **Automate the framework and focus on it**

"I'm no genius. I'm smart in spots—but I stay around those spots." — Tom Watson Sr., Founder of IBM

Whenever you have a decision to make, look through your mind to see if you understand it. Knowledge is not enough. Only act on what you understand or have a witness in your spirit about.

If you do not know enough to be useful in a certain area, delegate the decision to someone who has an understanding and results in that field.

One trap many people fall prey to is the need to diversify when they do not have a deep understanding. After the money starts coming in they immediately start buying stocks or real estate without assessing the opportunity cost. This is why marrying the right person and having the right mentors and business partners is important. Having the right advisors will anchor you and keep you in your circle of competence.

I get offers to do all kinds of projects and investments but I have learnt to stay in the place where I can be the biggest blessing.

THE SYSTEM FOR GETTING PAID MORE

Have you noticed it is easier to acquire more of what you already have? The world has a cliché that says the first million is the hardest. It's an incomplete truth but still valid in many ways. There is a principle I would like you to observe because so few notice it.

"To those who listen to my teaching, more understanding will be given. But for those who are not listening, even what little understanding they have will be taken away from them."-Jesus Christ (Mark 4:25)

It is important to know how the system works and how to get the results you desire from it. Jesus is teaching us here that without continuous personal improvement and development, an individual will lose what little they have. Haven't you seen people who get ahead in life and soon seem like they are moving backwards?

You get hired and paid based on what your value is and what the company thinks your contribution is worth. If you think your contribution is worth $100,000 a year but are getting paid $65,000 then either ask for a raise or quit to start a business or work for someone who appreciates your value.

If on the other hand your contribution does not equal the compensation you desire then create more value and tell the right people about it. Take some courses. Read more books. Ask for more responsibility so you can prove yourself.

When I started out in consulting, I **would insist** that part of my compensation be tied to the results I produced. Till this day I offer a full money back guarantee on all our workshops and events.

I believe this accomplishes two things:
1. Results are the best form of differentiation so it makes marketing your products and services easier. You can go to a client and say "I will help you achieve 10 percent growth in your business in the next 3 months" but many people say something like " I run an advertising agency". Sadly I have never heard an ad executive or freelancer ever start a conversation with growth benefits.

2. The testimonials will have more impact because others can see when others are prospering and would like to know what the source of the prosperity is. It also makes people trust that you are here to provide value not just for selfish reasons.

Conclusion

When I was an employee, I only wanted to work for an organization who paid a premium for results because that is something I could control. I wanted to work at a place where I knew exactly what to do to get to the next level. I did not want to leave my future to chance or in the hands of a boss who had not well defined system of rewards. Office politics and long years of experience are an inefficient way to the top.

If you do not get paid enough, resolve to do these 3 things

1. Add value to yourself (i.e. getting a deeper understanding: you can do this via books, apprenticeship, taking on more responsibility, courses)

2. Get results

3. Advertise the results to those who matter.

Very soon you'll be recognized and rewarded handsomely while other complain about the government, taxes and systems they do not understand.

For the entrepreneur and business owner
1. Focus on metrics that your clients care about. If I was a mother; saying you will help me lose weight is not as appealing as saying **you will help me lose so much weight that I can fit into the same jeans I was wearing before I had a baby**.
2. Develop yourself. Become a master at sales and marketing. Anyone can create a good product but few can sell. Read books on all those who are making billions in your industry.

3. Look for people who already have the clients you want to serve and show them your results. Propose a mutually beneficial promotion or deal in exchange for access to their clients. This will save you time and money. It will also help you not to concentrate on individual sales to get ahead.

DO YOU KNOW THE DIFFERENCE BETWEEN CUSTOMERS AND CLIENTS?

Why do clients buy more than customers do?

Last week I was having lunch with a client at a restaurant I have visited at least half a dozen times in recent years. My client had been there even more times and also knew the owner by name. We ate and worked there for about 2 hours. None of the staff knew our names or what we had ordered on our previous visits.

They had no data on us so they could not have recommended that we try their hot, juicy and delicious lamb or the banana and coconut smoothie. We were nameless and faceless economic transactions so they could not offer us any more value than their competitors across the street. They should have turned us from customers into clients but I am not sure they knew how to do so.

Do you know the difference between customers and clients?

Many retail businesses attend to customers while service entrepreneurs like lawyers, doctors and consultants usually describe the people they are engaged in helping as clients. At face value it is just a matter of choice which word you use but in thought and practice, it is infinitely better to have more clients than customers.

Customers buy once or twice and leave. They are nameless, faceless economic transactions on a balance sheet. It does not matter how much potential value you can give them or how much more they would buy if only you bothered to find out. Clients on the other hand are invaluable assets to a business. Clients are nurtured and made to feel special. We have conversations with clients about their children and even give them recommendations as to which barbershop or accountant to consider when the need arises. Clients are extended family members.

We do everything in our power to make sure they get more value for their money in the long term. This is not about making money once and letting them go, when we encounter a client, we keep them for life. Remember that clients are about the long game, customers are for today.

Conversation with event planner
I was advising an entrepreneur in the event and wedding planning space and noticed she was booking very few brides even though her value was practically unmatched. After the event, she hardly kept in touch with the brides so she did not even know which of them had younger siblings or friends who could be potential clients in a few years. I advised that the next time someone bought one of her services, she was to find out how many siblings they had, their ages and if they were engaged to be married in the near future.

Her assignment was to find a way to contact those potential clients and offer her services with the promise of a discount at least once a quarter till they got married. The plan was to not only get a client but the whole family as well. As long as she is in it for the long game, she will become a trusted consultant to each family she deals with. She will be sought after for every baby shower, birthday party or corporate event that happens amongst that group of people.

Conclusion

The biggest benefit and purpose of being in business is that it allows us entrepreneurs to be a bigger blessing to our clients and the world around us than anyone else. The entrepreneur who provides the highest value usually makes the most money and gets the most fulfillment. John D. Rockefeller reduced his profits by providing cheaper oil products than his competitors and in turn millions of people rewarded him with billions of dollars. He felt responsible for the quality of products being peddled in his industry and his clients paid him well for that mindset.

One way the restaurant I mentioned earlier should have converted us into clients by capturing our names, phone numbers or email addresses. In practice they can have clients write down these details on the bill or a separate sheet of paper. They can then use this information to email the menu, special events, new services, recipes or promotions to these clients in the future.

Remember that clients are about the long game, customers are for today.

Book recommendation: The Bible is the best book on how to run a business. IN this context, study 1 Corinthians 13:4-8 Amplified version on how to turn customers into clients.

WHAT I LEARNT ABOUT DRESSING WELL AND MAKING MONEY.

In college many of my mates were overly concerned about getting the right connections, references and investing in their appearance in order to get the right jobs and to get into the right meetings. Some people even dated certain girls because it would get them closer to the daddy or his world. After starting my first business I was invited to the home of a millionaire. I was obviously impressed and made him a customized t-shirt because that is what my connection to him advised.

Secondly I was running a t-shirt company so I brought the fruit of my labor. That meeting was of no benefit to either myself or the millionaire at the time. I had no big plan that would merit his time or investment and my business was not providing enough value to be worth his time.
Is there any way to dress well and increase your income at the same time?

Truly successful people who say their clothes have made them more money usually do not tell the whole story. They forget to mention that they have some value underneath the clothes. Many of these people are either really good at some skill or are running a business that creates value. We should always remember to focus more on what value you can provide than what you can wear. It seems simple enough but many are busy looking for connections instead of increasing their knowledge and skill so even after they meet the "right" person.

Looking back I would say that I was even better dressed than that millionaire that day but he had more value to provide than I did. Are there any other insights to dressing well?

HOW TO GET PEOPLE WHO MATTER TO VALUE YOUR OPINION

Before we begin, let me share a story from a man I respect deeply.

"It then happened for the third time before my wife stopped talking me into going again. She allowed me to make my decision. I had had enough. I went home and got busy. I neither called the bishop during this my period of total hands-on-ministry, nor went to see him again. I simply **bought all his books**, and a **thousand tapes** of the bishop. I read the books till they became a part of me. I listened to the tapes at home, in the office, and when I'm driving. I soaked myself in the work of the ministry.

We started many projects in our church, including setting up schools, orphanages, and the Daystar Leadership Academy. I didn't bother to call nor try fixing another appointment with his PAs.
Six months later, we met at the domestic wing of the Mortal Mohammed International Airport in Lagos, and you should have seen the look of surprise and happiness at the same time on the bishop's face.

> "This my son. Where on earth have you been?" Did you travel to Mars?" He hugged me so tight as if his life depended on it. He was all smiles. He started asking me questions about how ministry has been going, and I answered excitedly, with all the clarity he wanted.

We found a seat in the lounge and talked for about 30 minutes; because the flight was delayed by 30 minutes. He kept asking questions and I kept talking.

The next day, the bishop called me. He called me again after three days. From then on, seeing him became less cumbersome. That was how I became a regular keynote speaker at the Covenant University Special Programmed on Character Development and National Transformation. .

TAKE HOME LESSON
1. Deep calls unto deep. Men of destiny, men of purpose, men who are busy and occupied with their primary assignment on the earth can easily recognize themselves across a hall when they meet.
2. All things being equal, busy people love busy people. Busy people rarely love to associate with, or accommodate people who slow down their momentum.

3. So whenever you find yourself complaining about an apparent lack of attention from a busy person, the solution is to just go and get busy with your life and assignment.

First of all, discover your specific assignment, your niche, and grow in your influence. Get busy!

This is because recognizing each other when you're both at the top is far easier and effortless than recognizing each other at the crowded ground level. The high decibel of noise and purposeless activity of the crowd at the ground level, comprising of people of all sort of character and orientation will never allow that to happen."—Sam Adeyemi.

From the story above, you will notice that even though God was on his side, he still participated by adding value to himself and those around him. He developed himself spiritually, mentally and economically.

I am reminded of this verse by King Solomon,
"And I said, "Wisdom is better than strength, but the wisdom of the poor man is despised, and his words are not heard. Ecclesiastes 9:16"
A people who are not economically developed can be treated as slaves regardless of the nation they are in.

I have a few colleagues who work in public policy in Africa but many of them do work of little impact. Someone else makes the decisions while they type out stuff and fly to meetings. It is important to aim high enough to be at the decision-making table.

Get the Word of God in you and let Him guide you. Don't just show up and work 16 hour days and think you will make a difference in the world. Make sure you contribute more value to the organization than anyone in your paygrade (whatever that means).

If you are an entrepreneur, provide so much value that your clients will think your rates are too low for what you give them. They will brag about you to others.

Value that is recognized will attract money like a magnet. Value that is recognized will make you a decision maker. Till then your impact will be negligible and your voice will only go as far as the ears of a social media audience with no real power.

Give too much value and you will get that paper. You will be a bigger blessing to the world.

This is a lesson on how to get people to value your opinion. Now go out there and share your value.

THE PSYCHOLOGY OF BUSINESS STORYTELLING AND HOW TO EDUCATE YOUR CUSTOMERS

When Tommy Hilfiger was launching his first ad campaign via a billboard thanks to George Lois and Tommy's partner at the time, he may not have known that his audacious self-promotion of himself versus three of the most popular American menswear designers would turn into such a classic example of bravado and customer education. Tommy Hilfiger's ad not only made a statement, it taught the public that there was another trusted brand in menswear even they did not know it yet.

We like to buy from vendors that we trust. Trust comes from knowledge. We do not trust people or businesses we do not know. The more a buyer knows, the easier it is to spend. This is one reason why infomercials are so successful. They spend a lot of time telling you who, why, what, how and where you can buy their products.

In marketing, education always wins.
This works for healthcare as well as it does in the entertainment and even the retail industry. It is more than likely that you shop at retailers that you are more familiar with than those that you hardly see or hear about. Those who say advertising will cease to exist do not understand human nature. Think of your favorite musician or group.

After you came to like their music, you decided to find out more about them and can probably mention the names of all of their albums. This goes for sports teams and athletes as well. The more we know about them, the more we deify them.

One of the best books on this topic was written by Ogilvy on Advertising

Customer education defines the psychology of business storytelling.

The caveat here is that all knowledge is not created equal. Knowledge that we deem as acceptable, favorable or beneficial to us usually holds sway over our decisions. That detergent brand that tells you that Hydrogen Chloride was used in making their products may not cause you to whip out your wallet as easily as their competitor who tells you that they are using natural chemicals that make your clothes looking and smelling whiter, brighter and fresher.

See what I did there? The former was educating on features, the latter on benefits. The former was stating what is unique about them, the latter is stating how their uniqueness is going to impact the client's life.

How to educate your customers

Start off by making at least 90% of the information about them. Speak to their needs and tell them exactly how your product or service is beneficial to them. If you do not know what benefit your product provides then your customers will not know either. There are qualitative and quantitative benefits. In my practice I may use quantitative measures by saying "I will help you set up recurring income systems that will increase your revenue by 15% in the next 2 months."

For qualitative I may say "I will implement 4 marketing strategies that will give you peace of mind and allow you to be able to take one extra week of vacation time this year." Some businesses thrive better with qualitative over quantitative education.

Nike could sell you on the quality of the rubber soles and the toughness of their padding but it's more effective for them to sell buyers on how their shoes will help you to be more athletic just like the high jumping, fast running athletes in their ads. I often joke about how hardly anyone knows how many megapixels their smartphone's camera has because phones are sold more as lifestyle staples than gadgets for techies. The same goes for cars.

I would like to add that even if you cannot find something overtly beneficial to say, you can share awesome facts. Remember this?

At the time, no one was so boldly saying you could hold 30,000 songs in your pocket Information that wows people is good because it will spread by word of mouth faster and more organically.

Another example is in gaming. When I first heard that the Watcher 3 was made by a team, the quarter of the size of their competitors, I was intrigued. I also heard about how their budget was smaller and yet created an RPG that would take at least 200 hours to complete because of how deep it is. There may be other RPG's that are better but they have not bothered to educate me.

Conclusion

Tell your customers over and over again the following without being boring or overly technical. The better teacher will win even if she is selling something boring. Who would have thought a junk of metal sitting on four rubber tires could be seen as a collectible?

Why you are in the business of retail, food, real estate, fashion, computers, technology et cetera– What opportunities do you have a unique skill set for? Tell us

What you love about your job, products, industry– Share the emotional highlights and why you love going to work every day. This will also attract the right talent.

Your opinions, vision, mission, ideas, concepts and insights. —If growing up near a rice farm gives you a unique insight into Asian cuisine then please go ahead and share.

What products and services are available? — Tell your prospects about all your products. Variety to some people is a sign of how big your operation is and might build trust.

What the benefits of doing business with you are?

Where they can buy your products–Educate the public on when, where and how your products are distributed.

What materials went into the making of your furniture? –Talk about the grain, the weight, the source, the durability, how it fits into the customer's lifestyle.

Who else buys your cars and is happy with them–Get testimonials of your clients even if it's just one person.

How long it takes you to make that shoe, widget, application product and so on.

What happens behind the scenes? Do you have photos, journals, videos or info graphics to share?

Remember, the better teacher will attract more eyeballs and listeners.

COMPETITION OR MONOPOLY?

What metrics matter to your business?

When I left my last startup I started thinking about what we achieved and if we had done our best for our clients. My philosophy is that the best businesses for me are those where I can provide the most value to the largest number of people. This kind of thinking advocates that competitors are a nuisance who cannot or will not take care of your target market as well as you can. To adopt this mindset, you have to be committed to providing nothing less than the best value to your clients.

If you were the best surgeon in town, would you want your family to be treated by anyone else? The standard metrics used by other startups did not seem to please me. After reading both Titan and Peter Thiel's Zero to One, I realized what we had missed. We were using the wrong metrics.

Competition versus monopoly metrics

Metrics an entrepreneur and his team to know if they are doing productive work and if they are getting closer to their goals or targets. This is on the assumption that the business has targets that matter. Depending on the kind of business you want to have in 5 years, you may either be using what I call competitive metrics or monopoly metrics. I am in favor of the latter. While reading John D. Rockefeller's autobiography by Ron Chernow I realized what he set out to do. According to the author, Rockefeller had a sense of entitlement that drove him to think the oil business should be nurtured and preserved by him. He felt it was only right to protect consumers from all other competitors who would not give them the service they deserved. This mindset of course led him to control most of the oil production in much of the world for many years. On the other hand, he could have chosen to compete with others for customers. I'll explain why I agree with this mindset after I explain what the difference is.

Competitive metrics versus Monopoly metrics

Competitive metrics is when you measure your success according to stuff like sales, number of registered users, foot traffic, visitors to your website, revenue per month or whatever targets your sales people have been assigned.

Monopoly metrics are when you measure your business' success by what percentage of your market you are providing value. In contrast to purely competitive metrics, you are focusing of how big of the pie you are serving not just how many sales were made this quarter.

For example, a restaurant can boast of $10,000 in monthly sales from 1000 customers but is that business a success if the gross monthly sales of their market is $100,000 from 10,000 customers? This would mean that they only provided value to ten percent of the market. They allowed 90% of their family to be treated by another surgeon.
Not everyone agrees with me when I say this.

For some, this is being overly ambitious and I was told by one entrepreneur that too many customers would give you headaches. Lol.

Facebook decided to track active users when everyone else was tracking registered users. The latter is vanity while the former has made them the dominant force in social media globally. Focusing on registered users is like having a 100 vegetarians at your grilled pork soiree. The room may be packed but if no one is eating then it doesn't really matter.

HOW TO GET PEOPLE TO BUY WITHOUT SELLING TO THEM

By the time you get to the end of this post, you would have learnt how to plant images in someone's mind without forcing them to buy or even convincing them.

You will learn how to influence your ideal client to buy without selling overtly.

All I ask is that you use this technique of pre-supposition ethically.
Getting prospective clients to buy is both an art and a science. **Increasing sales is part influence and part metrics.** Take that as a working definition of marketing.
Marketing is the ability to attract buying customers using influence and metrics.

To influence someone to buy from you, the person has to think they are making the decision independent of your marketing or pitch.

No one likes to admit that the marketing works on them but their bank balance and the rising profits of successful companies says otherwise.

Pre-supposition is a way to influence someone by taking them further down the path to purchase before they make a conscious decision to commit.

Here is an example:
After we sign the papers, we will ship the goods in the next 24 hours. When you open the box, you will also receive our complimentary gift

for all our high paying clients. This gift also comes with a lovely rose gold watch that we will take the liberty to engrave with any name of your choice. Would you like it shipped to your home or office?

Notice what we did there?

Notice we weren't pushy or sale-sy?

Reading that would make you assume the client in question has already agreed to buy whatever we are selling. That is pre-supposition.

Let's break down the pitch.

1. **After we sign the papers**-this makes the assumption that the client has already decided to sign the papers. We innocently plant it in their minds that they will sign the papers.

2. **When you open the box, you will also receive** –this line does two things. First it pre-supposes that the client is going to receive a box and open it. Secondly, it plants an image of them already receiving and opening a box. They can already see themselves receiving something. Words are images hidden in letter form so use them tactfully and you can download images into a prospects mind very easily.

3. **Our high paying clients**–We called this person a high paying client before they even purchased anything. This is what I call Image Amplification. I will teach you more about this in an upcoming post. This technique is used by the military and in political campaigns. When you tell someone they are something that they are willing to become, their minds start considering the possibility that they are who you say they are.

Notice we didn't' say "when you become a high paying client". We already told them that they were a high paying client.

4. **Any name of your choice. Would you like it shipped to your home or office?**—the words "your choice" and "shipped to your home or office" are the coup de grace.

The former is a powerful way to make the decision personal. Everyone wants to feel in control of a buying decision so those words make it seem like they are the once who are in control of this decision.

The latter question now allows the prospect to decide whether this thing he has bought mentally should come to his home or office address?

See how simple it is to influence someone with pre-supposition?

Conclusion

Go back to the first sentence of this post and notice what I did there. I planted an image in your mind pre-supposing that you were going to read this to the end and that you were going to learn something.

Sneaky…I know…forgive me

Remember that this works best when you already know what the desires and end result of your prospect are.

Go ahead and use this technique and let me know if it works for you.

LATERAL THINKING IN BUSINESS (THE HELICOPTER VIEW)

Imagine that you and your family have managed to wriggle your way to the front of a jostling crowd in Disneyland, where the street parade is about to start. You and your children can't wait to see Mickey Mouse and his friends riding past on their beautiful floats. Donald Duck sails past and your children wave in excitement. Next comes Goofy, and then Pluto, and wow… is that Mickey coming up next? That's how we see life. We have a linear perspective and we see events unfold day by day. However, God's perspective is different. He has a "helicopter's view".–excerpt from Joseph Prince's Destined To Reign.

How Do You Apply Lateral Thinking To Your Business?

Start with this question, "What is the highest level of development I can create in this industry/product/delivery mechanism/system/strategy?"
The follow up question should be, "What is the highest level of value we can give our clients?" This will eliminate linear thinking. True innovation is when you provide more value than the client expects.

For example, Dell's innovation was not merely technical.

"At the time, no one had thought it possible to offer a totally "customized" PC at a competitive price. Nor did conventional wisdom believe that a customized PC offering could be scaled beyond a VAR business model.

Taking advantage of the Internet's disruptive forces, Dell's second innovation was to create a configuration order entry system making it simple for the average user to design a PC to their unique requirements. Dell also created a back end supply chain processes to build and deliver the completed PC to the customer's home or place of business within days, not weeks.

Dell is a great example showing how breakthrough business results don't necessarily have to be in the dimension of product innovation…3 types of innovations a company can explore and exploit:

1. **Product and Service Innovation:** For example Apple's iPhone
2. **Process innovation:** Often happen behind the scenes to provide customers with expedited and customized service at a price advantage – like Dell's PC configuration front and back end processes.
3. **Business model innovation:** Like Dell's model to sell computers directly to the end customer and skip the middleman.

Don't get me wrong, Dell computers were good, but really nothing exceptional that the rest of the competitors couldn't offer. In fact, value added resellers' primary differentiation was supplying its customers with custom configured PC's (hardware and software) to get specific jobs their customers needed to get done. What VAR's couldn't master though, was creating a business model and supporting processes to scale the way Dell did.

The then competing PC firms at the time (i.e. IBM, HP and Compaq), **could not respond to Dell's business model either because their business models were too depended on their distribution channels and mass production lines.**

Specifically, the competitors were both **"channel locked"** and operationally constrained (mass-customization was not built into their manufacturing processes).
It would have been too much of a risk for them to disturb their channel relationships and change their core production process. To do so would be to kill the goose that lays the golden egg. So they thought." Read the rest here.

Conclusion

In my consulting business most of my "competition" are into teaching the client what to do. My innovation was to give the client an exact plug and play marketing system. I take out as much confusion as possible and do the work for them. As simple as this seems, many people think it's too difficult to do.

Think about how to give the customer exactly what she wants regardless of what the norm is.

HOW YOU CAN DO BUSINESS LIKE A MISSIONARY

When missionaries go into a village, they take with them medicine, clothing, books, food and whatever the people in that community need.

Many times in a matter of months, the locals accept the missionaries as one of their own and some even name their children after them. Really effective missionaries can minister to over 5000 people in just a few weeks.

Many times these missionaries get more acceptance even though they require a translator to communicate than some of the local groups and even the government of that community.

How do they achieve so much?
It has to do with the mindset.

Missionaries go into a community with the intention of helping as many people as possible before they leave. Many times they know they have only a few months before they are transferred onto their next assignment so they do everything possible to create a monopoly of goodness in that neighborhood.

If they have medical supplies, they make sure they visit hundreds and sometimes thousands of homes many times on foot to deliver the drugs. Their goal is to make sure every need is met in that neighborhood.

This is the mindset of a successful entrepreneur.

To meet every need and desire we are uniquely equipped to supply.

What is the Monopoly of Goodness?

Business is an exchange of value. You give value to the market and it pays back in kind or cash or whatever you asked for.

It is deciding to be the biggest value provider in your market. It may not mean having the most clients at first since not all clients may be the ideal fit.

It does not necessarily mean having more products or features than everyone else.

It does mean however that among those who are a perfect product/market fit, your business is the highest provider of value to them.

To those clients, there is no one who cares more about them than you do and they will vouch for you and endorse you to everyone who will listen.

Conclusion

Decide to own your market by using the Monopoly of Goodness strategy.

Figure out what the market size is and decide to take ownership of all those who need your products and services.

Value demonstrated and promoted is the way to win.

How I Engineer Success Even Before I Pitch

My pitch was good. It wasn't great as far as sales pitches go but it was good.

I had showed them that we had done everything in the brief and even done extra work to impress them.

The people around the table were obviously impressed but I knew something was wrong by the looks on the faces of the CEO and COO.

The CEO started to tell us how she had 25 years of experience at some Fortune 500 companies and that she did not agree with our approach because even those companies did it differently.

Strike One!!
Her COO also started critiquing our designs and both of them got very condescending.

Strike Two!!
They started talking about technical details and analytical things that their staff may not have understood but I did.

I have a Computer Science degree and I understand the fundamentals of scientific analysis…but they did not know that.

You see, this was a purely creative project. It was a branding and design assignment so as most technical people do when they meet artists, they discount their work as just an embellishment to the real value.

The meeting ended and they were going to pay us about 5,000 less.

It was still good money but I was angry…not at the CEO and COO but at myself.

For two reasons…

These two things alone can give you immense leverage in every pitch.

1 The Principle of High Value Leverage

In business, both parties in a negotiation usually see it as a zero sum game….For me to win, the other party has to lose.

That mindset makes pitch meetings a militant affair when it's supposed to be two parties deciding on what is best.

One way to solve this is to go in with leverage and make the other person see the leverage even before you start.

Jesus said "No prophet is accepted in his hometown." Luke 4:24
To paraphrase in business terms, no businessperson is respected among his peers.

For example, when I was in high school, we were taught both core and advanced mathematics because I was in the Science track.

The best answers in my classroom were only mildly impressive to my classmates because it was not new to them.

My friends who were in the General Arts classes were only taught core mathematics so whenever I shared stuff with them about advanced math, they were thoroughly impressed.

Coming from the Science track gave me leverage in their eyes.

I could have been the worst advanced math student in my class but among those who only got to study core math, I was accepted.

It's the same in business.

When a lawyer speaks at legal conferences, she may get a few claps here and there but it's nothing to write home about.

However, when the same lawyer speaks at medical conferences, the doctors and chiropractors listen attentively and shower praise on her.

It's kind of like something I read about our legal industry.

Apparently practicing law in New York City is regarded as tough. It's said that if you excel as a lawyer in New York, you can succeed anywhere.

I read that junior lawyers who left with New York City firms on their resumes usually got huge promotions in other states because those firms gave them leverage in other states.

This may be similar to what gave Marissa Mayer the job at Yahoo. She is known as the youngest Fortune 500 CEO and some say her credibility as a young executive at one of the most successful companies in the world (Google) made it easier.

How does this apply to you, the next time you pitch something?

It's important to be pitch a business or individual who does not have your value and can see the difference.

In the aforementioned meeting, I had no leverage because CEO's of energy companies do not generally consider Branding Consultants (that's what I was at the time) as partners of high value.

What I should have done was–
1 to make them know the caliber of the person pitching them,
2 to show them examples of work we had done for even bigger clients
And
3 analytical proof that we understood their business and could help them.
Remember this and you will accelerate your success even before you start.

2 Pitch as a Helper, Not a Beggar

Look at your timeline on Instagram, Facebook or Twitter. You will notice that most of the businesses and brands are trying to get you to buy something.

It is usually just photos of what their product can do or why you should take advantage of it now or miss out on some time-bound discount.

They are like beggars holding out their signs asking for a handout.

Contrast that with a business that tells you exactly what THEY CAN DO FOR YOU and the myriad of ways YOU CAN BE HELPED if you buy their product.

It's very difficult to say no when you know what's in it for you. This was another mistake I made going into that meeting.

I pitched as a vendor not a value added service.

They saw me as one of those who wanted their business not as someone who was there to help them do better.

Conclusion

Remember to always go into a meeting with leverage and try to communicate it even before the pitch starts.

The best kind of leverage is the kind that the other person views as an asset and not a liability.

Secondly, ALWAYS pitch people you can truly help and let them know what's in it for them.

P.S

You may have noticed that in each post I share how the psychological fundamentals matter in marketing and sales. I do this on purpose because strategies and tactics come and go but human behavior is very predictable.

ABOUT THE AUTHOR

JEFFREY A. MANU is a marketing strategist, entrepreneur and speaker.

He is the founder of GrowingStartup; a media and technology company in Silicon Valley. He loves Jesus Christ and spends much of his time spreading the light of the Gospel.

He lives in California with his wife.

This book is designed to provide information that the author believes to be accurate on the subject matter it covers, but it is sold with the understanding that neither the author nor the publisher is offering individualized advice tailored to any specific portfolio or to any individual's particular needs, or rendering investment advice or other professional services such as legal or accounting advice. A competent professional's services should be sought if one needs expert assistance in areas that include investment, legal, and accounting advice.

This publication references performance data collected over many time periods. Past results do not guarantee future performance. Additionally, performance data, in addition to laws and regulations, change over time, which could change the status of the information in this book. This book solely provides historical data to discuss and illustrate the underlying principles. Additionally, this book is not intended to serve as the basis for any financial decision; as a recommendation of a specific investment advisor; or as an offer to sell or purchase any security. Only a prospectus may be used to offer to sell or purchase securities, and a prospectus must be read and considered carefully before investing or spending money.

No warranty is made with respect to the accuracy or completeness of the information contained herein, and both the author and the publisher specifically disclaim any responsibility for any liability, loss, or risk, personal or otherwise, which is incurred as a consequence, directly or indirectly, of the use and application of any of the contents of this book.

At the time of this publication, the author is in discussions with Stronghold Wealth Management to enter into some type of business partnership. However, at this time, the author is not an owner of Stronghold, nor does he have any type of referral for compensation relationship.

In the text that follows, many people's names and identifying characteristics have been changed.

www.ingramcontent.com/pod-product-compliance
Lightning Source LLC
Chambersburg PA
CBHW070231190526
45169CB00001B/151